WHAT ARE THE
CHANCES?

WHAT ARE THE
CHANCES?

Risks,

Odds, and

Likelihood in

Everyday

Life

Bernard Siskin

Jerome Staller

David Rorvik

Crown Publishers, Inc.
New York

Special thanks to Morton Klein for bringing us all together

Published by Crown Publishers, Inc., 225 Park Avenue South, New York, New York 10003.

CROWN is a trademark of Crown Publishers, Inc.

Manufactured in the United States of America

Library of Congress Cataloging-in-Publication Data

Siskin, Bernard R.
    What are the chances? : risks, odds, and likelihood in everyday life
    Bernard Siskin, Jerome Staller, David Rorvik.
        p.   cm.
    1. Risk.   2. Probabilities.   I. Staller, Jerome.   II. Rorvik,
David M.   III. Title
HB615.S58   1989
306—dc19   88-38959
                                                                CIP

ISBN 0-517-57260-5

Design by Lauren Dong

10 9 8 7 6 5 4 3 2 1
First Edition

This is dedicated to our wives
Barbara and Michele
and our children Allison, Eric, Howard, Shara, and Chad
who have borne with us in the face of terrible odds.

Contents

Introduction

Chance It

If you can make one heap of all your
*   winnings*
And risk it on one turn of pitch-and-
*   toss,*
And lose, and start again at your
*   beginnings*
And never breathe a word about your
*   loss, . . .*
Yours is the Earth and everything that's
*   in it,*
And—which is more—you'll be a
*   Man, my son!*

—RUDYARD KIPLING, "IF"

Or a Woman, as the case may be. In any event, step right up and take your chances. Life is a series of dangers and opportunities, promises and perils, gains and losses, fortunes and failures. Life *is* chance.

This book, while it is certainly meant to entertain—and sometimes astonish and even frighten—

is also meant to educate, challenge, and perhaps encourage new ways of thinking and behaving. In our experience, when people see the elements of chance that form the fabric of their lives starkly quantified—and sometimes provocatively juxtaposed—they frequently make startling gains in perspective and insight, gains that enable them to productively change their minds, their hearts, their behavior.

Or you may just decide to change your job, your geography—or your spouse. Some may finally be motivated to shed those extra pounds, take up a new sport, and stop wasting time waiting for an invitation to appear on "The Tonight Show." Some may stop cheating on their taxes; others may start.

Many will discover that they have been worrying needlessly about risks and chances that, in reality, are extremely remote, while finding, at the same time, that they have been overlooking perils that pose imminent—and sometimes disastrous—threats. Some will abandon long-held aspirations and begin to nurture new ones.

Many others will feel less alone. Unloved, unmarried, unpromoted, still a virgin? You've got company—and the risk statistics will tell you just how much and what your long term chances are.

Everything we do, everything we believe, everything we feel entails a significant degree of chance. Deciding *not* to take a chance is sometimes the riskiest thing of all. Ultimately, as Rudyard Kipling suggests, what matters most is not so much *what* we chance but *how* we chance it. With the right attitude, and a dash of humor, we can sometimes make even our greatest losses our greatest gains.

Some Long Shots

....

What are my chances of being struck by lightning in my lifetime?

1 in 600,000.

....

What are my chances of appearing on "The Tonight Show"?

1 in 490,000—a bit better than your chances of being struck by lightning, but we still don't advise you to hold your breath.

....

What are my chances of winning a lottery grand prize with a single ticket?

WHAT ARE THE CHANCES?

You'd do better—much better—to wait for lightning to strike or for Johnny Carson to call. Looking at all the major state lotteries, your chances of winning one with a single ticket come to 1 in 5,200,000.

S*ome*
Good Bets

2

Compared with other dangers, how risky is air travel?

Not very risky at all. Every time you simply fall down, for example, you are 6 times more likely to be killed than when you travel in an airplane.

How likely am I to still be alive in another year?

If you are an average American you can count on it with a high level of confidence. The average American is 99.8 percent likely to live at least one more year.

WHAT ARE THE CHANCES?

Given the prevalence of terrorism around the world, just how risky is overseas travel?

Overseas travel is very safe. Your chances of being killed by terrorists overseas is 1 in 650,000. Better you should worry about being struck by lightning or by being killed by Americans in Baltimore. (The chances of the latter happening are greater than 1 in 4,000!)

Remember to Change Your Shorts

You Never Know When You'll Be in an Accident

If I drive a lot, on which day of the week is it *most* important that I wear clean underwear?

If you are determined not to humiliate your mother—or yourself, make sure your undergarments are particularly fresh on Saturday—far and away the most dangerous day of the week on which to drive. You can be considerably more careless about your hygiene on Monday and Tuesday, both nearly twice as safe as Saturday.

If you want to get right down to the hours in which you are at greatest peril while driving, be aware that you are *most* likely to be killed in an automobile accident between the hours of 10 P.M. and 2 A.M. Those hours are more than twice as risky as the hours between 6 A.M. and 10 A.M.

WHAT ARE THE CHANCES?

How much safer are large commercial airlines than smaller commuter lines?

The big boys are 500 times safer.

....

My plane has just taken off—what are the chances that it will crash and someone will be killed?

We hate to scare you while you're in flight, so order a double, sit back, and steady yourself. There's a 1.6-in-10-million chance your flight will crash and someone will be killed.

....

What toy is the riskiest?

The two-wheeled peril, the bicycle, accounts for an astounding 385,000 emergency-room visits among children under 15 in the U.S. each year. Spills account for almost all of this trauma.

....

In terms of fatal accidents, which month is safest, which riskiest?

Remember to Change Your Shorts

Save the money you'd spend on swimming suits and outboards for ice skates and scarves. July—by an enormous margin—is the most fatal month for accidents, February the most benign.

....

In terms of serious injury, is it riskier to be a professional boxer or a professional baseball player?

Those who campaign to halt boxing because of its "brutality" should hang up their gloves and grab a bat instead. Dodging balls turns out to be far more perilous than dodging fists.

....

In terms of physical injury, is it riskier to be a farmer or a big-city cop?

Compared with the perils the typical farmer faces, even inner-city boys in blue might as well be on vacation in Hawaii. Farm injuries are among the most prevalent and violent experienced by any occupational group.

....

In which state is it most dangerous to drive or ride in an automobile? Which is the safest?

We'd have guessed California, but the most dangerous turns out to be New Mexico. All that wide-open space must be intoxicating. Meanwhile, wouldn't you know it, the safest state is sensible New Jersey.

....

How much more likely am I to be involved in an automobile accident if I drive or ride in a small car than if I drive or ride in a large car?

Not at all more likely. On the contrary, the largest-sized cars are more often involved in fatal accidents than are the compacts and subcompacts.

....

Will cross-training in several sports at once decrease my risk of exercise-related injury?

No. It will *increase* it substantially. Triathletes who compete in running, swimming, and cycling have been shown, in some surveys, to suffer up to nearly 3 times as many injuries as those who train for and compete only in swimming. Those who compete only in running or cycling also have far fewer injuries.

....

Am I more likely to die from an accident related to firearms or one related to electric current?

Remember to Change Your Shorts

The firearms are about twice as likely to kill you accidentally.

....

If I'm an American Indian, am I more or less likely to die in an accident?

One study indicates that 1 in 5 Indians die in accidents, compared with 1 in 17 in the general population.

....

What are the chances I will be injured in an automobile accident this year?

About 1 in 75, looking at the population as a whole. Motor vehicle crashes kill nearly 50,000 people and injure about 3.4 million people annually. The cost of all this carnage to the U.S. economy is nearly $75 *billion* each year.

....

In those states that have seat-belt laws, has the risk of injury or death in automobile accidents really been reduced?

Yes. These laws have resulted in nearly 7 percent fewer deaths and 10 percent fewer serious injuries.

In those states where the speed limit has been increased to 65 miles per hour, has there been any appreciable increase in road fatalities?

The best study to date indicates a negligible increase of 1 percent. Researchers in West Germany, incidentally, have declared the country's 5,000-mile Autobahn system, which has no speed limit, "the safest road" in Germany. It accounts for only 4 percent of the nation's auto accidents—and most of those occur in construction zones where there are temporary speed limits.

. . . .

Have tougher state and local laws in force since 1980 related to drunk driving reduced alcohol-related auto fatalities?

There was, in fact, an 11 percent decline in alcohol-related traffic deaths between 1982 and 1985, but then in 1986, the last year for which we have complete data, alcohol-related auto fatalities rose by 7 percent. Some authorities believe that public disapproval of drunk driving, more than the laws themselves, inhibited this activity; now that the disapproval has peaked and is not being expressed as strongly, these officials reason, drunk driving is making a comeback.

. . . .

Who are at highest risk of not using seat belts, men or women?

Men. Also among the least likely to use seat belts are people under age 30, minorities, the poor, and drunk drivers.

....

What is the risk that a teenager will not use automobile seat belts?

56 percent.

....

How effective are seat belts in preventing fatal injuries?

40 percent to 50 percent when properly used.

....

Is it riskier to drive in Japan or the U.S. from the standpoint of fatalities?

Japan is about 75 percent riskier.

....

Is it riskier to drive in Spain or Japan?

Spain is more than twice as risky.

WHAT ARE THE CHANCES?

Are motorcycles really much more risky than cars in terms of fatal accidents?

Motorcycles are nearly 14 times more likely to kill you.

....

Are rural dwellers, suburbanites, or city dwellers the most likely to be killed in non–motor vehicle accidents?

Country folk are almost twice as likely as suburbanites to be thus felled. City dwellers fall in the middle range. And the range is quite broad: the risks in the country are 34 percent above the national average and 31 percent below those in the suburbs.

....

I am planning a 500-mile trip. What's the safest way of getting to my destination—car, plane, or train?

Call the depot. Your chances of being killed on the train are only 0.15 in a million, about half what they'd be on a plane. Your chances of being killed if you drive the 500 miles are 31 times greater than if you trust in Amtrak.

....

Am I at greater risk of having a fatal accident in New York City or Los Angeles?

Remember to Change Your Shorts

The risk of fatal accident in Los Angeles is almost twice what you will encounter in New York. Even L.A., however, looks like a safe haven compared with some smaller cities such as Tampa, Florida; Jacksonville, Florida; and Phoenix, Arizona.

....

Is my child at greater risk of being killed or disabled by accident, by drugs, or by childhood disease?

Accidents account for more death and disability among children than drugs and all childhood diseases combined.

....

How dangerous is the sort of diving accident where the victim plunges into too-shallow water headfirst?

Very dangerous. This type of accident leaves half of all its victims paralyzed from the neck down.

....

What are the chances that as a beginning skier I will be injured on the slopes?

Not too high. 1 in 300.

WHAT ARE THE CHANCES?

In which line of work am I most likely to have an occupational injury?

The lumber industry. You're 20 times safer being a stockbroker, the safest of all jobs in terms of occupational injury.

....

Which part of my body is at greatest risk in a work-related accident? My fingers, legs, or trunk?

Trunk—injured in 32 percent of all accidents. Fingers and legs are injured in only 14 percent and 13 percent of all accidents, respectively.

....

Among household cleaning items/appliances, does a washing machine or a hot iron pose the greater peril in terms of human injury?

From the safety point of view, better to leave that ring around the collar. The washing machine causes more injuries than any other cleaning item in home use. Bleach comes in second, the iron third.

....

How risky is the bathroom—from the standpoint of accidental injuries?

Remember to Change Your Shorts

25 percent of all in-home accidents (amounting to 270,000 injuries) occur in the bathroom each year. Falling in the shower or tub is the major culprit.

....

Am I more likely to burn something or break something this year?

You're 2.7 times more likely to break your leg, arm, or neck than you are to suffer a burn serious enough to require medical treatment.

....

What are the chances I'll be injured/killed in a residential fire this year?

The risk of injury is 8.1 in 100,000; the risk of death is 2.1 in 100,000.

....

What are the chances I'll be injured/killed in a motel/hotel fire this year?

The risk of injury is 1.6 in a million; the risk of death is 3.6 in 10 million. You're considerably safer sleeping at Howard Johnson's than at home.

WHAT ARE THE CHANCES?

I have a deadly fear of snakes. What is the chance that the bite of a poisonous snake will be the cause of my death?

2.9 out of every 10 million people succumb to the serpent. Stay out of the tall grass.

....

Which dogs are most likely to bite?

German shepherds, followed (in this order) by chow chows, Airedales, and Pekingese.

....

Which dogs are most likely/least likely to assume friendly attitudes toward children?

There are many exceptions, of course, but the experts say that mastiffs, boxers, Newfoundlands, bloodhounds, Bernese mountain dogs, Samoyeds, Labrador retrievers, Chesapeake Bay retrievers, beagles, Boston terriers, English cocker spaniels, and pugs are most likely to get along with the little people. *Least* inclined to tolerate kids are those two sweeties, the St. Bernard and the old English sheep dog, along with the Alaskan malamute, the bull terrier, and (proving that small doesn't always take to small) the toy poodle.

Marriage, Divorce, Sex, and Other (Romantic) Mayhem

....

4

What are my chances of marrying if I am 18 years old or older?

64 percent.

....

If I want to marry a very young woman, where are my chances the greatest?

From the legal standpoint, Rhode Island, where females may marry at age 12!

....

Is the risk of never marrying greater for men or women?

Men stalwartly shoulder the greater risk here, at least during their younger years. Men are 37 percent more likely to re-main single—but only up until age 55. At that point the situation shifts a bit, with women over age 55 some 5 percent more likely never to have married.

....

What are the chances I will marry someone of another race?

Less than 1 in 50.

....

What are the current chances that my spouse and I will have three or more children?

Under 11 percent; in 1960, the chances would have been greater than 20 percent.

....

If I'm a professional woman, how likely am I to find romance on the job?

Very likely—about 55 percent. And the office romance is likely to last longer than those that originate in singles bars or health clubs.

....

How likely is it that, if we don't divorce, both my spouse and I will live to celebrate our fortieth anniversary?

Pretty good. In fact, 2 out of 3 marriages (that avoid divorce) will thus endure. This is considerable improvement over 1900, when only 1 in 3 marriages continued for forty years without a visit from the Grim Reaper.

....

What are the chances I will still be a virgin when I am 16?

50 percent.

....

How risky is it for a woman to ask a man for a date?

Not very. In fact, 71 percent of all datable men say they would welcome a woman taking the dating initiative.

....

Are the overall chances that I will marry going up or down with time?

Down. In a little more than a decade there has been a remarkable reduction in the incidence of marriage. In 1972, 141.3 of every 1,000 single women between ages 15 and 44 married within the calendar year. By 1985, the last year for which these data have been compiled, the rate had dropped to 94.9 women. If this trend continues, the National Center for Health Statistics estimates, only 70 percent of American women will ever walk down the aisle. (In 1972, 87 percent of all American women could count on marriage.)

....

Am I likely to find happiness in marriage?

Married people, according to a recent survey, still count themselves happier than unmarried people—but the happiness gap between the two groups is narrowing significantly. It seems that more and more people are finding themselves just as happy to be unmarried. A dozen years ago there were 20 percent more married men (between the ages of 25 and 39) than unmarried men who described themselves as "very happy." Today there are only 5.7 percent more "very happy" married men. Among women, the differential has slipped from nearly 30 percent a dozen years ago to only 12 percent today.

....

In what month am I most/least likely to get married?

If you are afraid of marriage, hole up somewhere alone in the month of June. Emerge in January—the month of fewest marriages.

....

If I am a college-educated white woman and I have not married by the time I reach age 40, how likely is it that I will *ever* marry?

Marriage, Divorce, Sex, and Other (Romantic) Mayhem

Less than 1 percent. If a woman has not married by the time she is 35, there is only a 5 percent chance she will marry.

....

I have my eye on a 45-year-old man who has never married. What are the chances I can lead him to the altar?

Throw some more mothballs on your wedding gown. Your chances of bagging this one are only 1.2 percent.

....

At what age are people most likely to marry?

For both men and women, ages 25 to 29 are the high-risk years for marriage. In second place for women are the years 20 to 24 and for men the years 30 to 34.

....

As a girl who wants a guy, at which age am I most likely to snag one, based on their overall availability?

Alas, you'd practically have to rob the cradle. Under the age of 14, boys outnumber girls, but only by 5 percent. After that it's a woman's world, with the men in constant relative decline. At retirement age, there are only 68 men for every 100 women. Your best bet is to get your man as early as possible.

WHAT ARE THE CHANCES?

I'd like to marry a younger man. What are my chances?

About 33 percent overall—considerably better than they were ten years ago.

....

If I'm 21 and not married, should I be worried?

No. The median age of both males and females at first marriage is steadily moving higher. For females it's now nearly 23, for males, 24.

....

What are the chances that a woman, divorced or widowed between the ages of 15 and 44, will remarry within one year, three years, five years?

7 percent remarry within one year, 35.7 percent within three years, and 49.4 percent within five years.

....

What are the chances, overall, that I'll remarry after divorce?

78 percent for women, 83 percent for men.

Marriage, Divorce, Sex, and Other (Romantic) Mayhem

What are the chances my marriage will end in divorce?

About 50 percent.

....

If a guy marries at age 15, how much more likely is it that he will get divorced than a man who marries at age 24?

Not at all more likely. The just-past-puberty groom is more likely to stay married than the world- and woman-weary 24-year-old.

....

I'm a teenager whose parents have just divorced. Will this unpleasant experience make me more or less likely to divorce someday?

The offspring of parents who divorce are themselves more likely to divorce than are the children of those who remain married. For females this greater likelihood amounts to 50 percent, for males, 23 percent.

....

Having risked and carried through with divorce, are men or women more satisfied with their newly regained single status?

WHAT ARE THE CHANCES?

It's the divorced or separated woman who does most of the sighing—but these are sighs of relief. Some 85 percent of divorced or separated women say they are happy with their single status; only 58 percent of the men are likewise content.

....

What are the chances my marriage will endure forever?

Slim. The median duration of marriage in the U.S. is only seven years.

....

In which regions of the country are couples most/least likely to divorce?

Most likely in the South and the West, least likely in the Northeast and Midwest.

....

Are better- or lesser-educated women more likely to divorce?

Education and divorce are inversely related, meaning the more you have of one, the less you have of the other. The less educated divorce not only more often but earlier.

Are better-educated or lesser-educated women, divorced or widowed between the ages of 15 and 44, more likely to re-marry?

The less education a woman has the more likely she is to remarry.

....

Will "cohabitating"—living together without being mar-ried—improve our chances for a lasting marriage if we finally do tie the knot?

That's the common wisdom in many circles, but a recent study of Swedish couples indicates this is not the case. In fact, among those who live together in Sweden before marriage, there is an *80 percent greater chance of divorce.* Swedish social trends tend to precede those in the U.S. by about ten years, and sociologists here believe that cohabitation in the U.S.— which has quadrupled in the past decade—will similarly re-sult in diminished regard for the "holy" state of matrimony in this country. Couples will still marry, but they will not feel as "bound" by their vows as those who did not cohabitate.

....

Is a person who marries at age 24 more likely to end up getting divorced than a person who marries at age 34?

Yes, considerably more likely, and this is true for both men and women. The divorce rate is particularly high for people who marry in their twenties. The rate steadily declines with age thereafter.

....

As a divorced woman, what are the chances I'll collect alimony?

About 6 percent of all divorced women collect alimony. Among divorced women who remarry, less than 1 percent still collect alimony from their former husbands.

....

I'm an about-to-be-divorced father. What are the chances my child will live with me rather than with the mother?

13.3 percent.

....

Are those who have "loved and lost" more likely to die than those who have never married?

The divorced/separated are at lower risk of dying next year than those who have never married.

....

Do marriage and divorce have any influence on heart attack risks?

Yes. Marriage seems to reduce the risk for males. Married men have a 6 percent lower chance of dying from a heart attack than do separated/divorced males and a 23 percent lower risk than men who have never married. For women, marriage is also protective against heart attacks—unless marriage leads to divorce or separation, in which case the risk of heart attack soars to 37 percent above the risk experienced by women still married and to 33 percent above those women who never marry.

....

Is marriage good for immunity?

Yes, according to an Ohio State University study. The immune systems of married women were found to be functioning better than those of unmarried women. *Happy* marriages produced even healthier immune systems.

....

Does going beyond a normal college education—into postgraduate work—have any effect on a woman's marriage prospects?

Yes, it dims them considerably. Women with postgraduate college education are three times less likely to marry than are women with no more than high school educations.

WHAT ARE THE CHANCES?

Is a woman, divorced or widowed between the ages of 15 and 44, more likely to remarry in some regions of the country than in others?

Yes, such women are more likely to remarry in the South than in other regions. Women in the Northwest are about 50 percent less likely to remarry than women in the South.

....

What are the chances I'll be giving somebody a Valentine's Day card?

High. Among American adults, 78 percent buy—and presumably send/give—a Valentine's Day card.

....

What are the chances that my son will spend more on a gift or flowers for his sweetheart on Valentine's Day than he will on something for me on Mother's Day?

Sky-high. Retailers say men are more stingy when it comes to Mother's Day gifts, reckless by comparison when it comes to Valentine's Day gifts and flowers. Some 64 million roses (70 percent of them red) are sold on Valentine's Day.

....

In view of the AIDS risks, I'm interested in knowing if single women between the ages of 18 and 44 are more or less sexually active than they used to be.

More active. Some 76 percent of these women report that in 1987 they were sexually active, up from 71 percent in 1982, according to researchers at the Alan Gutmacher Institute and Ortho Pharmaceutical Corp.

....

Are women who read a lot of romance novels more likely to be lousy lovers?

On the contrary. The common wisdom is that such women "sublimate" sexual urges by reading these novels, but a recent study indicates that the romance novel addict has sex 74 percent *more often* than those who read more staid—and apparently less stimulating—material.

....

Which sexually transmitted disease am I most likely to contract?

That depends upon your individual sexual preferences and activities, but, overall, chlamydia is, far and away, the more frequently transmitted sexual disease—with at least 4 million cases annually. There are about 2 million cases of gonorrhea, 1 million cases of genital warts, half a million cases of genital herpes, and 85,000 cases of syphilis transmitted each year. There are about 45,000 cases of sexually transmitted disease per day, with an annual total of more than 16 million.

In terms of their failure rates, are U.S. or foreign condoms the best?

Buy American. Recent tests indicate a 12 percent failure rate for the domestic models, a 21 percent rupture rate for the sleek foreign jobs.

....

Does having sex the night before an athletic event reduce one's chances of winning that event or performing well in it?

This myth was recently put to bed by a study at Colorado State University. Pre-event abstainers did no better than indulgers. Stamina, agility, reaction time, muscle power, and all the other variables were virtually the same in both groups tested.

....

How likely is it that, as a woman between ages 40 and 44, I'll have sexual intercourse more than twice a week?

35 percent.

....

What are the chances the single woman I have my eye on right now approves of premarital sex?

50 percent.

Marriage, Divorce, Sex, and Other (Romantic) Mayhem

What are the chances my marriage will be of the "shotgun" variety—the result of pregnancy?

About 15 percent of all marriages are thus initiated. A recent study reveals that such marriages are not as shaky as previously believed. More than a third of them are still intact after ten years.

....

What are the chances a baby will be born to parents who aren't married?

22 percent of all U.S. babies are born out of wedlock, a figure that continues to escalate.

....

What are the chances that, as a teenager, I'll never have sex?

Not great. Some 70 percent of teenage girls and 80 percent of teenage boys have sex at least once during their teen years. By age 16, half of all teenagers have had at least one sexual encounter.

....

Does contraception failure (leading to unwanted pregnancy) occur more often in one region of the country than another?

WHAT ARE THE CHANCES?

Don't ask us why, but yes. In fact, the risk of this happening is twice as high in the West as in the Northeast—at least among the couples studied (all in their first year of marriage).

....

What are the chances my teenage son thinks it's okay for a husband to rape his wife or for a man to rape his date?

One survey indicates that 86 percent of boys age 13 to 15 think it's okay for a husband to rape his wife; 24 percent say it's okay for a man to rape his date if he's spent "a lot of money" on her.

....

If I'm dating a woman who could become pregnant, what are the chances she is using no contraception whatsoever?

12 percent.

....

I'm a teenage girl planning to have sex with a teenage boy. What are the chances he will use a condom?

Only about 20 percent. Be aware that there are about 1 million teenage pregnancies in this country each year.

What are the chances my teenage lover will have a sexually transmitted disease?

Pretty good, unfortunately. 1 in 7 carries such an infection.

....

In which English-speaking country am I most likely to find an eligible man?

In England itself, for the first time in history, men outnumber women. There are presently 240,000 more men than women in the 15 to 29 age group.

....

Is there risk from a person who has herpes but currently has no active lesions?

Yes. The risk is actually slight—individuals without active lesions are shedding virus only about 0.5 to 1.5 percent of the time. But since there is no way of telling when shedding is occurring, those with herpes are advised to use condoms whenever they have sex.

....

What are the chances my bride will be a virgin?

20 percent or less. If you had married 25 years ago, the chances would have been 50 percent.

....

In what nation of the Western world is the risk of unintended pregnancy the greatest?

The home of Mom and apple pie—the United States. In view of this it is not surprising that the U.S., among Western nations, also has the highest rate of abortion per capita.

....

Is hair on a guy's face or his chest a bigger turn-on for women?

Hair on the face is risky. The majority of women say they now prefer their men clean-shaven. On the other hand, they prefer hairy to smooth chests.

....

As a woman with average breast size, I wonder what is the chance men will find my better-endowed sisters more attractive?

You're in luck. The majority of men now say they actually prefer average-sized breasts to larger ones.

Marriage, Divorce, Sex, and Other (Romantic) Mayhem

Are men or women at greater risk of becoming stuck on themselves?

Behold the strutting male, 28 percent of whom consider themselves handsome; only 13 percent of all women think they are pretty.

....

To what extent is not having blond hair risky for a woman looking for a man?

It's not risky at all, provided you have long brunette hair, which men now say they find equally attractive as long blond hair.

....

As a man, I'm wondering if it's riskier to have short or long hair, curly or straight hair when it comes to attracting the opposite sex.

Long straight hair poses the greatest peril at the present time. More women prefer short curly *dark* hair on a man than any other type of hair.

....

In view of all the adverse publicity about the negative effects of too much sun, is the once-popular tan coming to be regarded as a fashion don't? Is it losing its sex appeal?

No. The once-popular tan is the still-popular tan. A majority of both men and women still find a tan a turn-on.

....

If I want better sex, is the purchase of a water bed a good investment?

It's a bit shaky. Only 33 percent of those who buy water beds say sex is better on them.

....

As a woman who works for the federal government, what are the chances I will be sexually harassed by male coworkers/supervisors?

In two separate surveys, about 40 percent of women working for the federal government claimed such harassment had occurred.

....

I'd like to know, as a woman, what is the risk that I will one day have unwanted intercourse with a man simply because he continually argues with me and nags me to go to bed with him.

Our answer will, unfortunately, dishearten many women and encourage certain men: 25 percent.

Marriage, Divorce, Sex, and Other (Romantic) Mayhem

What is the risk that a woman will have unwanted sexual intercourse at some point in her life because a man has threatened her with physical force or actually used it to coerce her?

9 percent.

....

What is the risk that a woman will have unwanted intercourse with a man who uses his higher authority at work to coerce her?

2 percent.

....

Are men or women at higher risk of encountering longer waits at public rest room facilities?

Women definitely have to stand in line longer. That's because women take longer. In fact, according to a recent study, they take an average of 34 seconds longer than men to use a rest room. Women average 79 seconds, men 45.

On the basis of these findings, one researcher has concluded that the "toilet ratio" should be altered, from its roughly 50–50 status currently, to 60–40, with the women getting the excess. The state of Washington is already paying heed, building more toilets for women along its highway system. Meanwhile, next time you're in an airline (or anyplace the sexes use the same rest rooms) and have to "go" in a hurry, you'll know which line to choose. As a rough rule of thumb, just remember that, in this context, it takes 7.5 guys to equal 10 women. Toilet-wise women in a hurry will remember that too.

5

Crime and Punishment

In what month am I most likely to be shot to death, poisoned, or strangled?

Merry Christmas.

....

What are the chances I will be murdered this year if I live in a small city?

If you live in a town of 12,658 people, you *could* be the one.

....

What are the chances I will be the victim of a serious crime in my lifetime?

1 in 20.

WHAT ARE THE CHANCES?

How much more likely am I to be robbed than murdered?

Hold on to your wallet. 500 times more likely.

....

If I live in a city of 250,000 or more, how much more likely am I to be murdered than if I live in a city of fewer than 10,000 people?

6.4 times more likely.

....

What are the chances that the person who murders me is someone I know very well?

58 percent.

....

If I am raped, robbed, or assaulted, what is the likelihood that the assailant is of my race?

About 80 percent overall.

....

Are men or women more likely to be the victims of violent crime?

Crime and Punishment

Men—and they are also 5 times more likely to be arrested for committing violent crimes.

....

Are the rich at higher risk of having their homes burglarized?

No. Those with family incomes of less than $25,000 annually are about 30 percent more likely to be burglarized than those with family incomes of $50,000 and up.

....

Am I more likely to be murdered or to kill myself?

You're more likely to do yourself in (12 out of 100,000 suicides versus 8.8 out of 100,000 murders).

....

Am I at higher risk of being the victim of a violent crime in the daytime or at night?

Violence is as likely to befall you in broad daylight as it is under cover of darkness, with one exception: rape. Rapists still prefer to strike at night; you are 2.7 times more likely to be raped at night.

....

Does having a lot of people in my household reduce the risk of a burglar succeeding in making off with our goods?

No. In this context, at least, there is no safety in numbers. The risk of successful burglary actually *increases* the more people there are in your household. The chances of successful burglary in a 6-plus household, for example, are about 65 percent greater than in a single-person household. So don't start advertising for a roommate—at least, not for that reason.

....

What are the chances an attempted rape will *not* succeed?

48.9 percent.

....

Are you more likely to be murdered over matters related to money or romance?

While it may be true that money can't buy you love, it *is* more likely to cost you your life: you are 13 percent more likely to be murdered over an argument concerning money than over disputes related to "another man" or "another woman."

....

Is arguing risky?

If you value your life, yes. Approximately 40 percent of all murders occur during arguments.

....

If I'm robbed, how likely is it I will lose $1,000 or more?

Only 5 percent of all robberies net that much.

....

What are the chances I will be injured while being robbed?

About 30 percent.

....

As I grow older, am I at greater risk of being robbed?

No. From age 24 on, your chances of being robbed actually diminish steadily. Those 65 and over are about 6.5 times *less* likely to be robbed than those 20 to 24.

....

Is the risk of being robbed greater for males or females?

Males are twice as likely to be robbed as females.

Am I more likely to be raped in the street or inside a building?

In the street (26.3 percent of all rapes). Another 25.5 percent of rapes occur in the victim's own home or on the victim's property.

....

What is the risk I will be raped, robbed, or assaulted by someone I know?

Approximately 43 percent, 12 percent and 42 percent respectively.

....

Will taking self-protective measures when someone attempts to rob me increase my chances of being injured?

Yes, by 12 percent.

....

Will taking self-protective measures when someone attempts to rob me reduce the chances of that attempt being successful?

Yes, by 52 percent.

Crime and Punishment

Does marriage in any way reduce the chances of my being a victim of violent crime?

Yes. Single men and women are more than 3.5 times more likely to be thus victimized than are married men. Divorced/separated women are at even greater risk than single women.

....

Is a car that I rent or own more likely to be stolen?

Apparently you are more careless with cars that don't actually belong to you. The rate of thefts for rental cars is more than double that of non-rentals.

....

How likely is it that if someone tries to snatch my purse they will get away with it?

Prepare to go shopping—for a new purse. The likelihood is 80 percent.

....

Are the risks of being raped different for women who are married/single/divorced-separated?

Yes. Those who are divorced/separated are about 12 percent more likely to be raped than those who are single and about 7½ *times* more likely than those who are married.

WHAT ARE THE CHANCES?

Which cars are most likely to be broken into?

Volkswagens—thieves love their radios. The theft claim rates for two Volkswagen models (the GTI and the Cabriolet convertible) are almost 70 times greater than that of Mercury's four-door Lynx, which is at the bottom of the thieves' wish list. Midsized domestic models, in general, don't appeal to car thieves. In addition to Volkswagens, car thieves tend to favor Saabs, Peugeots, and Porsches.

....

Do car alarm systems really reduce risk of theft?

Yes. Insurance companies report 30 percent fewer claims for vehicles with these systems.

....

What are the chances that, as a first offender, I'll offend again and wind up back in prison?

29 percent.

....

Is it riskier for society, from the financial point of view, to send a criminal to prison for life or execute him/her?

Crime and Punishment

Contrary to popular belief, according to a survey by the New York State Defenders Association, it presently costs society a lot more to execute than imprison. In New York it costs about $600,000 to imprison someone for life. To litigate a capital punishment case through the lower and appeals courts typically costs the taxpayers nearly $2 million.

....

Is violent crime in America escalating as fast as I think it is?

It's not escalating at all. Even though nonviolent crime in some sectors (such as government) seems to be increasing rapidly, the overall rate of violent crime in this country has actually declined slightly in recent years, according to the Justice Department.

....

Are the elderly at greater/lesser risk than the young of being crime victims?

The elderly are only half as likely as the young to be crime victims. Moreover, crimes against the elderly have declined 50 percent in the last fifteen years.

....

If I go to prison, what are the chances I'll find someone there conversant with Shakespeare?

Not good. The average prisoner hasn't gotten beyond the tenth grade.

....

Is it financially riskier for society to release repeat offenders early or build more prisons?

The idea that we can't afford to keep repeat offenders in prison has been challenged by a Justice Department study of 2,190 inmates in California, Texas, and Michigan. The study concluded that while it costs society $25,000 per year to keep a prisoner incarcerated, the tab for letting one go early is about $430,000 per year. Almost all repeat offenders return to lives of crime, and the $430,000 is calculated on the basis of average victim losses, police, probation, court, and private security expenses. Looked at in another way, the Justice Department study finds that for every 1,000 offenders kept in prison, society saves a net $405 million. We may be looking at a new high-growth industry.

....

Is a woman more likely to go to prison today than she was a decade ago?

Yes. Between 1976 and 1986 there was a 138 percent increase in female imprisonment (compared with a 94 percent increase for men).

Crime and Punishment

What is the risk that the angry-looking man on the freeway in the vehicle next to mine will take some aggressive, dangerous action if he thinks I've crossed him somehow?

In one recent survey in freeway-choked Southern California, 43 percent of all men questioned admitted they had taken such actions out on the road.

....

What is the risk that the driver next to me on the freeway is toting a gun?

Nobody knows for sure. One recent study of this issue found that a quarter of all those motorists questioned said they know someone who carries a gun in his/her car.

....

Is a young person more likely to meet a violent end in a big-city ghetto or in the most isolated parts of the West?

The "frontier" apparently still exists. A number of studies show that young people (ages 15 to 24) are at a considerably greater risk of violent death in the rural West than they are in even the toughest big-city ghettos. Among reasons given: lack of community cohesion, boom/bust economies typical of the rural West, little or no law enforcement, excessive drinking, "individualism" leading to a tendency to deal with problems outside the law. Low-population counties in Utah,

WHAT ARE THE CHANCES?

Arizona, Nevada, and New Mexico are the riskiest for youth; there the violent death rate among white youths exceeds even the death rates for black youths living in the highest crime urban areas.

....

Is ethics in government on the skids?

Some statistics suggest that this is the case. Whereas there were 53 federal officials under criminal indictment in 1975, there were 563 in 1985; 43 federal officials were convicted of crimes in 1975, 470 in 1985 (the last year for which figures were tallied).

....

If I'm on Death Row, am I more likely to be black or white?

White, 57 percent; black, 41 percent. On a per capita basis, however, far more blacks than whites end up on Death Row.

....

If I'm on Death Row, what's the risk I'll actually be executed this year?

Slight. Last year there were about 2,000 individuals on Death Row, but only 25 were executed. That's 1.25 percent.

Crime and Punishment

What is the risk a police officer will be killed in the line of duty?

3.8 in 10,000.

....

What is the risk a police officer will be assaulted in the line of duty?

15.8 in 10,000.

....

If I'm tried for homicide, what are the chances the jury's verdict will be guilty?

Slightly less than half: 49.4 percent.

....

If I'm found guilty of homicide in federal court, what are the chances I will actually be imprisoned?

70 percent.

....

If I'm tried in federal court for forgery/counterfeiting, what is the risk of a jury finding me guilty? And if I am found guilty, how likely am I to actually have to spend time in prison?

There's an 80 percent chance you will be found guilty, but only a 49 percent chance you'll go to prison.

....

Are those found guilty in federal court of burglary or of embezzlement and fraud more likely to actually serve time in prison?

Convicted burglars go to the big house 75 percent of the time, while embezzlers and frauds "go up" only 37 percent of the time.

....

Apart from the obvious—loss of valuables and possible injury—are there hidden risks in being burglarized or robbed?

Yes. Nearly 20 percent of those robbed or burglarized are so traumatized by the event that they move to a new location shortly afterward. More than 14 percent buy guns.

....

In which room of the typical American home is the risk of violence the greatest?

The bedroom.

Crime and Punishment

Are men or women at greater risk of killing themselves with poison?

Poison is the self-destruct method of choice used by women—in 58 percent of all female suicides. Men prefer firearms—using them in 64 percent of all male suicides.

....

In which city is one most likely/least likely to be subject to violent crime?

Most likely in Detroit, where there are 2,375 violent crimes per 100,000 population. Least likely in San Diego and San Antonio, where there are 630 violent crimes per 100,000 population. Put another way, the risk of violent crime is 4 times greater in Detroit than in San Antonio or San Diego.

....

In which city am I most likely to be the victim of theft?

Keep both eyes on your belongings in Dallas.

....

Where is a woman most likely/least likely to be raped?

The risk of rape is highest in the West, where the rate is about 40 percent higher than in the Northeast, which has the lowest per capita rate of rape. Alaska is the rape capital, with 73 rapes per 100,000 population—a rate more than six times that of North Dakota, which has the fewest rapes per capita. Next to Alaska, Nevada has the worst rape record. Next to North Dakota, Maine has the best record.

....

Where am I most likely/least likely to be murdered?

The South produces the most stiffs per capita via murder, the Midwest the fewest. Washington, D.C., which, in most categories, qualifies as the crime capital of the U.S., has a murder rate *31 times greater* per capita than North Dakota, where you are least likely to be murdered. Maine and Vermont are also relatively murder-free. Texas and Nevada follow D.C. for homicides—but even these states are relative safe havens compared with D.C.

....

Where is the risk of being robbed greatest/least?

Greatest—you guessed it—in Washington, D.C., where the risk is about double that of California, itself a very high-risk state for robberies. The risk is lowest in South Dakota and Montana.

....

Where am I at greatest/least risk of having my car stolen?

Crime and Punishment

Overall, your risk is highest in the Northeast, lowest in the Midwest. You're most likely to lose your wheels in Washington, D.C., followed closely by Massachusetts and Michigan. You're about ten times less likely to have your car stolen in South Dakota than in D.C.

....

Where is a woman most likely to commit a murder?

Most likely, of course, in Washington, D.C. Second most likely in Nevada. Third most likely in Alaska.

....

In which region of the country are law-enforcement officers most likely to be killed/least likely?

Most likely in the South, least likely in the Northeast.

....

Am I more likely to be killed by a blunt object or by strangulation?

Helmets are advised; you're more than twice as likely to experience the blunt object. You're even more likely, however, to be killed by a gun or a knife.

Am I more likely to be robbed in my home or out on the street?

You're six times more likely to be robbed on a street/highway than in a residence, two times more likely to be robbed in a residence than in a convenience store, and nine times more likely in a residence than in a bank.

....

Am I more likely to be killed by another human or by some other animal species?

According to one study you are 34 times more likely to be intentionally done in by a fellow human than by all of the other animal species combined (excluding infectious organisms).

....

Is a man or a woman at higher risk of serving a long prison sentence?

Men serve, on average, about thirty months in prison; women typically serve eighteen months.

....

What crime classified as "serious" by government authorities am I most likely to be arrested for?

Larceny/theft.

Crime and Punishment

Which crime classified as "nonserious" am I most likely to be arrested for?

Driving while intoxicated.

....

Are men or women more likely to be reported in child maltreatment cases?

More than 60 percent of those reported for maltreatment of children are women.

6

Doc, What Are My Chances?

How safe is circumcision?

Pretty safe. But 200 people lose their lives as well as their foreskins from undergoing this procedure each year in the U.S. alone. Thousands more require emergency medical intervention and "corrective" surgery.

If I'm a male infant, where am I most likely to retain my foreskin—Britain, Australia, Canada, or the U.S.?

Britain—where 98 percent of all male infants now get through childhood "uncut." (The circumcision rate in Britain used to be very high: it seems that the medical "need" for it evaporated when the National Health Service decided to stop paying for the surgery.) 78 percent of all male infants remain connected with their foreskins in Australia, 76 percent in Canada, and only 60 percent in the U.S. Some doctors, incidentally, now perform foreskin reconstruction.

. . . .

As I grow older, am I more or less likely to catch cold?

Less likely. After age 65, you have only a 14 percent chance of catching cold in any given year, compared to a 20 to 76 percent chance for younger age groups.

. . . .

Are males or females more likely to catch colds?

Boys more than girls, women more than men.

. . . .

How risky are medical X rays?

Most authorities consider them, overall, safe. But you should be aware that there are more than 45,000 fatal cancers induced by medical X rays in the U.S. each year.

Doc, What Are My Chances?

Are some X rays riskier than others?

Yes. All medical X rays pose some peril, but the amount of radiation you are exposed to in some radiological studies of the gastrointestinal tract, for example, is 90 times that you are exposed to during a typical dental X ray.

....

In which state is it financially riskiest going to the hospital?

From the standpoint of cost, Massachusetts, where the average cost per stay is more than $4,100. Lowest average cost per stay is in Mississippi, where the bill comes to a little over $2,000.

....

Is my VA doctor what/who he claims to be?

According to a report in the *New England Journal of Medicine,* 17.7 percent of 650 Veterans Administration doctors who claimed to be board certified were not.

....

If I'm having surgery, at what time of year are complications most likely to follow?

It's been a joke in medical circles for some time that July is a bad time to have surgery because that's when teaching hospitals typically bring in new interns and residents. It turns out this may *not* be a joke. A study at the Veteran's Administration Medical Center in Denver recently found that complication rates for medical treatment, and for surgical procedures in particular, escalate from 20 percent in June to 50 percent in July. Perhaps you'll want to opt for a tan, rather than surgery, in July; it *may* be safer.

....

What is the chance that what I'm going to see the doctor about will turn out to be of little consequence?

Among the complaints presented to primary-care physicians, 30 to 60 percent, according to various surveys, have little, if any, health significance.

....

If my child is short at age 3, does that mean he/she is at risk of being short as an adult?

There is a good correlation between height at age 3 and height in adulthood. You can calculate how tall your child will be in adulthood by measuring the child at age 3 and multiplying by 1.87 for boys and 1.73 for girls.

If I sleep with my pet, is it riskier for me or the animal, from the standpoint of passing on disease?

The risks are about equal—very low for both human and pet (provided we're talking about cats and dogs). Tuberculosis and ringworm are among the diseases that, in rare cases, can be traded.

....

What are the chances I'm covered by private health insurance?

76 percent.

....

Are males or females more likely to be hospitalized?

Even though men are injured more often than women, females are 15 percent more likely to be admitted to hospitals—even when admissions for childbirth are excluded.

....

What are the risks of smoking during pregnancy?

Among women who smoke regularly, there is up to a 35 percent higher risk of death to the unborn baby in the eight weeks before birth—and the same increased risk to the baby in the first week after birth. Smoking is not recommended at any time during pregnancy—but risks are especially high when smoking continues after the fourth month of pregnancy and when more than ten cigarettes are smoked per day.

....

If I'm pregnant, is there any risk in my working with a video display terminal?

Perhaps, according to a recent study conducted by researchers at the Kaiser-Permanente Medical Care Program in Oakland, California. Women who use these displays for more than 20 hours each week during the first three months of their pregnancies are nearly twice as likely to have miscarriages. Whether the displays themselves or job-related stress (or both) are responsible remains to be determined.

....

Are boys or girls at greater risk of dying before birth?

Boys have a 25 to 30 percent greater risk of dying in the womb.

....

What are the chances I will die while giving birth?

Doc, What Are My Chances?

The death rate for white females is currently 5 per 100,000 live births—10 times less than it was in 1950. For black females, however, the current death rate is nearly 21 per 100,000—more than 4 times that of the white rate.

....

What is the risk that my baby will have to be delivered by cesarean section?

21.1 percent overall. The risk increases with age to more than 35 percent for expectant mothers ages 35 and up.

....

What are the chances my baby will die in its first year?

A lot less than they were back in 1950. Today the death rate for white infants is 9.4 per 1,000 live births, about one-third of what it was in 1950. For black infants, the death rate now is 18.4 deaths per 1,000—which is about 2.5 times less than it was in 1950.

....

Which is more risky, legal abortion or pregnancy/childbirth?

You are 10 times more likely to die during pregnancy/childbirth than during a legal abortion (8 in a million, versus 80 in a million).

WHAT ARE THE CHANCES?

Are legal abortions appreciably riskier later in pregnancy, compared with early in pregnancy?

Yes. The risk of the mother dying increases twenty-four-fold if she has the abortion after the thirteenth week of pregnancy (as compared with having it in the first nine weeks of pregnancy).

....

What are the chances my hysterectomy wasn't necessary?

Up to 30 percent of all hysterectomies are unnecessary, according to some experts.

....

Is a woman more likely to have a hysterectomy in the U.S. or in England, France, or West Germany?

The U.S. woman is 2 to 3 times more likely to have a hysterectomy than women in those other countries.

....

What are the chances my pregnancy will result in twins—or more?

Slightly over 2 percent.

Doc, What Are My Chances?

Are white or black women more likely to have multiple births (twins, triplets, etc.)?

Blacks are about 25 percent more likely to have multiple births.

....

Do my chances of having a multiple-birth pregnancy increase or decrease with age?

Increase. The multiple-birth rate for women 35 to 39 is nearly triple that of females under 15 (9.6 per 1,000 live births versus 27 per 1,000 live births among the older women).

....

What is the risk that a married woman (15 to 44) will be infertile?

Excluding the surgically sterilized, the risk is about 14 percent.

....

Due to infertility problems I want to have a baby via an embryo transfer procedure. What are the chances of success?

17 percent that you will become pregnant by this method, 11 percent that you will deliver a live baby.

....

Is there any risk in wearing tight-fitting Jockey shorts?

An increased incidence of infertility has been reported among men who habitually wear tight-fitting pants and/or Jockey shorts. This reduction in fertility is reversible upon going back to looser-fitting clothing. Those in a hurry to fertilize have actually been advised by some doctors to put their rocks on ice—but only for brief periods.

....

Is there any truth to the rumor that anesthesiologists and jet pilots are more likely to give birth to girls?

Yes, various studies over the years have confirmed that men who are exposed to a lot of toxic chemicals, high heat, unusual pressures (jet pilots, deep-sea divers) are more prone to father girls than boys. Apparently these stresses kill off the slightly smaller and presumably less hardy male-producing sperm more easily than they do the larger, hardier female-producing sperm.

....

Are men or women more likely to contract fatal illnesses?

Men.

Doc, What Are My Chances?

Are men or women more likely to have nonfatal illnesses?

Women are much more likely to have these illnesses.

....

What are the chances I will experience a dozen or more symptoms of ill health in any given year?

Excellent. One study shows that the typical American experiences about 80 symptoms of illness per year. These include such things as headaches, fatigue, runny noses, rashes, palpitations, and diarrhea.

....

Overall, are the risks of dying from cancer increasing or decreasing?

Increasing—by more than 9 percent since 1950. Most of the increase is attributed to lung cancer.

....

What are the chances I will survive at least five years if I have just been diagnosed as having cancer?

Your chances are as follows, depending upon the type of cancer: pancreas, 3 percent; esophagus, 5 percent; lung, 13 percent; stomach, 17 percent; leukemia, 33 percent; ovary, 38 percent; kidney and rectum, both 50 percent; colon, 53 percent; cervix, 66 percent; prostate, 70 percent; breast, 74 percent; bladder, 75 percent; skin, 80 percent; oral cavity, 83 percent.

....

Am I more likely to die of diabetes or cancer?

You are about 14 times more likely to die of cancer.

....

Am I at greater risk of dying in an accident or from heart disease?

You are approximately 5 times more likely to die from heart disease.

....

Am I more likely to risk an unproven medical treatment if I have arthritis or cancer?

36 percent of all arthritis sufferers have tried unproven remedies, while only 15 percent of all cancer patients have resorted to these.

....

Has the risk of dying from breast cancer gone down since routine breast X rays to detect early cancers were recommended?

No. The death rate has remained nearly unchanged for almost twenty-five years. Health officials say the reason for this is that most women are not having regular breast X rays. A recent survey indicates that 62 percent of all women 40 or older have never had a breast X ray; 17 percent said they didn't even know such cancer-detecting breast X rays (called mammograms) exist. Federal health officials have been recommending for some time that women age 40 to 50 have these X rays at least once every two years and annually after age 50. They believe breast cancer mortality can be reduced 30 percent if women follow these recommendations. There are currently about 135,000 new breast cancer cases and 42,000 breast cancer deaths annually.

. . . .

What are the chances a precancerous cell change will go undetected after a single pap smear?

1 in 3, according to some authorities.

. . . .

Do more people die on the highways or from prescription drug adverse reactions annually?

Far more die from drugs than traffic, about 125,000 versus 50,000.

. . . .

Are men or women more likely to have hemorrhoids?

WHAT ARE THE CHANCES?

Men are 5 percent more likely to reach for the Preparation H.

....

Are men or women at greater risk of being constipated?

Women sport that telltale pinched look 2.53 times as often as men.

....

Are men or women more likely to have bunions?

The women won't get a kick out of this answer, since they suffer this affliction 3.35 times as often as men do. Whatever happened to sensible shoes?

....

Do men or women suffer more often from high blood pressure?

Women, contrary to popular belief. Men, however, die more often from damage caused by this disease.

....

Migraine headaches have been characterized as the curse of the rich and/or the smart. Does the incidence of migraine increase with socioeconomic status?

No, in fact the opposite is true. The risk of migraine goes down as you move up the socioeconomic scale.

....

What are the chances I don't know my cholesterol level?

Among U.S. adults, 87 percent, according to one survey, 93 percent, according to another survey.

....

What are the chances my cholesterol level is too high?

According to figures some think are too conservative, 25 percent of all Americans have cholesterol levels so high they are at serious risk for coronary heart disease.

....

Does lowering cholesterol really reduce the risk of heart disease? By how much?

Yes, it does—and dramatically. For every 1 percent reduction in your blood cholesterol you earn a 2 percent reduction in the risk of coronary heart disease according to an advisory panel of the National Institutes of Health. If Americans would reduce their blood cholesterol levels by even 10 percent, 100,000 fewer of them would die of heart disease each year.

I've heard that body shape can be a risk factor for some serious diseases? Is that true?

Yes, men are at increased risk of heart disease, diabetes, and stroke when their waists are the same size (around) or even bigger than their hips. Women are also at significantly increased risk when their hips are *not* at least 20 percent larger than their waists. Upper-body fatness in men has been associated with a sixteen-fold increase in diabetes risk.

....

How likely am I to develop high blood pressure?

Pretty likely. More than 40 percent of us have reached the boiling point. Blacks more often than whites have this affliction. (But see next question.)

....

What are the chances my "high blood pressure" has been misdiagnosed?

According to a study at Cornell University Medical Center, as many as 21 percent of those currently on lifelong medication for high blood pressure (hypertension), don't have this condition at all. Instead, they are suffering from harmless "white-coat hypertension," which means their blood pressure is elevated only when the doctor measures it. Younger women are believed to be at the highest risk of this misdiagnosis.

Doc, What Are My Chances?

Are blacks or whites at greater risk of dying of heart disease?

Blacks. Black men are about 320 percent more likely to die of heart disease than white men, and black women are about 50 percent more likely to die of this disease than white women.

....

What is the *least* I can exercise and still significantly diminish the risk of cardiovascular disease?

As little as twelve minutes three times a week—provided the exercise is of the aerobic variety.

....

When is jogging more hazardous than helpful?

Jogging in major urban areas, where air is polluted, is often more harmful to health than no exercise at all.

....

I'm thinking of buying an exercise bicycle. Will it be a waste of time and money?

Probably—but only because you're not likely to use it regularly. Only about 17 percent of those who purchase exercise equipment actually use it more than once a week.

WHAT ARE THE CHANCES?

What are the chances I will stick with my new exercise program?

Don't retire your easy chair just yet. A number of studies indicate that 50 percent drop out before they are six months into sweat. Fully 25 percent don't even start their first session!

....

In what part of the country am I most likely to live longest?

If you're male, point your horse west. Male mortality is a significant 11 percent lower in the Pacific states (Washington, Oregon, California, Alaska, and Hawaii). If you're female, head south to Kentucky, Tennessee, Alabama, or Mississippi, where your chances of dying are an even more impressive 17 percent below the national average. For both males and females, the mortality statistics are deadliest in the mid-Atlantic states.

....

In which part of the country are women at least/greatest risk of dying of breast cancer?

The risk in New England is 35 percent *below* the national average. The "east south central" area (Kentucky, Tennessee, Alabama, and Mississippi, otherwise friendly territory for women) is where the risk is greatest—30 percent higher than average.

Doc, What Are My Chances?

Am I more likely to die next year if I live in a central-city area, the suburbs, or out in the country?

Your chances of dying are greatest in the central city. The suburbs, however, prove more conducive to life than the country.

....

In which developed countries do males have the longest/shortest life expectancies?

Longest in Japan (74.2 years) and Sweden (73.1), shortest in Singapore (68.7), Ireland (68.8), and Scotland (69).

....

In which developed countries do females have the longest/shortest life expectancies?

Longest in Japan (79.7) and Norway (79.4), shortest in Czechoslovakia (74.3) and Cuba (74.9).

....

Among those living in the U.S. at the present time, is the risk of dying next year greater if the individual was born in the U.S. or in a foreign land?

The "home grown" folk are at greater peril of not being around next year. Foreign-born males have a nearly 20 percent lower risk; foreign-born females have a 3 percent lower risk.

....

How much better is it being a woman than a man when it comes to life expectancy?

White women live 10 percent longer than white men (78.7 years versus 71.8 years); black women live 13 percent longer than black men (73.7 years versus 65.3 years). If it was a man who coined the term *Vive la difference,* he should have given it a little more thought.

....

How much greater is the risk of dying of heart disease for a man than for a woman?

About double.

....

Which disease is most likely to kill me?

Cardiovascular disease. It kills more than *1 million* Americans annually.

Doc, What Are My Chances?

If I have a heart attack, how likely is it that it will kill me?

About 60 percent of those who have heart attacks die instantly or within one hour of the attack.

....

How much of a risk is radon?

This odorless radioactive gas, a product of nature that wafts into dwellings from underground rocks, is currently blamed for about 13,000 lung cancer deaths yearly. Millions of families, according to government estimates, are being exposed to dangerous levels of this gas. Smokers exposed to radon are at a risk of developing lung cancer that is 10 times greater than radon-exposed nonsmokers.

....

I'm thinking of having my diseased knee joint replaced with an artificial one. What are the chances the operation will succeed?

Very good: 9 out of 10 artificial knee joints are still functioning properly 11 years post-op.

....

What are my chances of coming down with polio?

WHAT ARE THE CHANCES?

Virtually zero today—compared with 22 percent in 1950.

....

In which cities are health risks the lowest?

A recent study, based on a variety of federal and private data, identified these cities as the ten "healthiest" cities: Honolulu; Seattle; Minneapolis/St. Paul; Milwaukee; Boston; Pittsburgh; Greensboro, North Carolina; Richmond, Virginia; Rochester, New York; and Scranton/Wilkes-Barre, Pennsylvania.

....

In which city am I most likely to enjoy the longest life expectancy?

Honolulu, where the typical resident enjoys three extra years over the national average making it to 77.

....

In which city are my chances of surviving a heart attack best?

One recent study says Seattle, where average ambulance response time is said to be only three minutes and where nearly 25 percent of the entire metropolitan population is said to be trained in emergency CPR (cardiopulmonary resuscitation)!

Doc, What Are My Chances?

In which states am I most likely/least likely to be able to get a hospital bed when I need one?

The hospital occupancy rate is greatest in New York, Washington, D.C., and Connecticut. It's far easier to get a bed in low-occupancy Nevada, Wyoming, and Montana.

....

How likely is it my friends will call me "Four eyes"?

Pretty good. Nearly 52 percent of all Americans end up wearing glasses, women more often than men: 57 percent versus 46 percent.

....

How likely is it that my hair will be white by the time I'm 50?

Averaging men and women together, there is a 50 percent chance that half of your hair will be white by the time you reach age 50. Whites begin graying at an average age of 34, blacks at an average age of 44.

....

Does snoring pose any risk to health?

A study has appeared in the *British Medical Journal* that suggests snorers are at risk of more than just unhappy or angry spouses who can't sleep through the racket. Snorers, in this study, were found to be at *twice* the risk of non-snorers of heart disease and stroke! This remarkable increased risk held up even after the researchers took into account such other high-risk factors as smoking, alcohol consumption, obesity, and high blood pressure.

....

Who is more likely to be less physically active than average, the rich or the poor?

The rich. In fact, the more money you make, the less physically active you are.

....

Is being poor a health risk?

Definitely. The U.S. Centers for Disease Control recently released a report that shows that the rich live significantly longer than the poor. The rate of potential life lost among those individuals who make less than $12,100 per year is more than twice that of those who make more than $19,300 per year.

....

Which risk factors are the most important in terms of chronic disease and premature death?

Use of tobacco and alcohol, high blood pressure, "overnutrition" (obesity and high cholesterol), poor primary health care, especially during pregnancy, and situations that increase the risk of injury (certain jobs, sports, for example). Some 70 percent of potential years of life lost are attributed to these six factors.

....

Are there any hidden risks in blood transfusions, apart from infectious agents?

A startling recent study at the Rochester Medical Center found that 43 percent of colon cancer patients had recurrences of their cancers following blood transfusions while only 9 percent of those who did not have transfusions had recurrences.

....

If I am a man who never shaves, do I face any particular health peril?

Those who face *you* are more likely to feel imperiled. By not shaving for your entire lifetime you would save yourself 3,350 hours—but you'd have to be careful not to trip over your approximately 30-foot-long beard. You'd also have to worry about putting on an extra pound—in hair—every sixteen years. Yes, someone did actually figure this all out—to the inch and the ounce: the good folks at Gillette Safety Razor Co.

....

What are the chances I'll be exposed to harmful levels of noise at my place of work or in the course of carrying out my job duties?

About 5 percent are exposed to levels of noise sufficient to damage hearing.

....

Am I more likely to die of AIDS or the flu?

The flu poses a far greater threat than AIDS to the general population. Influenza still kills about 70,000 Americans *each year*. It took more than *seven* years for AIDS to kill that many.

....

What is the risk of contracting AIDS from a blood transfusion?

The risk has been estimated at between 1 in 30,000 and 1 in 200,000. You are far more likely to contract some other disease—such as hepatitis or malaria—from blood transfusions.

Does AIDS or measles pose a greater risk to the world population?

Since AIDS emerged in 1981 it has killed fewer than 100,000 people worldwide; measles in that same period has killed more than 14 million.

....

Does AIDS or cigarette smoking pose a greater peril to society?

Smoking. The Centers for Disease Control state that diseases caused by cigarette smoking kill approximately 1,000 Americans every day. Cigarette smoking kills as many Americans in five weeks as AIDS has killed in ten years.

....

Which is more infectious—syphilis or the AIDS virus?

According to the Centers for Disease Control, syphilis is 400 to 500 times more infectious than the AIDS virus. The infection rate for the latter is less than 0.1 percent male to female and less than 0.05 percent female to male for heterosexuals not in a high-risk group (such as intravenous drug users).

Risky Business

Money, Education, Jobs, Success, Failure

7

Will I be able to indulge in more wretched excess if I become a psychiatrist or an orthopedic surgeon?

There's more money in bones than brains—a lot more. The typical orthopedic surgeon makes twice as much as the average shrink, who may or may not suffer from penny envy.

In which state am I most likely to be employed?

Massachusetts.

How much more likely is a female today to be a doctor, dentist, lawyer, or engineer than her mother was?

WHAT ARE THE CHANCES?

Doctor: 5 times; lawyer: 15 times; dentist: 25 times; engineer: 30 times.

....

Which spaces am I most likely to land on in a Monopoly game?

Illinois Avenue and B&O Railroad—and so will your competitors, making these "best buys" on the board.

....

What are the chances that the main reason I will go to college is to make more money?

71.3 percent. Up from 49.9 percent in 1971, when the majority of students cited presumably loftier reasons for seeking college diplomas.

....

What are the chances I will seek a college education in order to develop "a meaningful philosophy of life"?

Only 39 percent. Down from 82.9 percent in 1967. As free-lance writer Molly McCloskey notes, "Four out of five freshmen now choose Wall Street over Walden Pond."

If I'm a married man, what are the chances I've lost control of the family purse strings?

Pretty good. Women control the checkbook and pay most of the bills in 75 percent of all American households.

....

Will learning how to play golf increase my chances of becoming a top executive?

We can't say for sure, but be advised that 69 percent of 200 top executives surveyed by *Golf Digest* profess to be duffers who play more than 12 rounds of golf a year. So far as we know, however, Harvard has not yet made Golf 101 part of its MBA curricula.

....

Looking back over the past *five* years, what were the riskiest/ least risky investments?

Least risky were stocks (24.1 percent return) and bonds (19.7 percent); most risky were U.S. farmland (which actually lost 7.8 percent in value) and oil (which lost 11.8 percent in value annually).

....

Looking back over the past *fifteen* years, what were the riskiest/least risky investments?

WHAT ARE THE CHANCES?

U.S. coins yielded the highest annual return over the past fifteen years—18.8 percent. By contrast, the annual return on diamonds over the past fifteen years comes to only 4.1 percent. Oil, U.S. stamps, gold, and silver all yielded more than 10 percent annually over the fifteen years, stocks yielded 8.6 percent (not as good as Treasury bills at 9.2 percent or Old Masters at 9.2 percent), housing returned 8.2 percent, U.S. farmland 6.3 percent, and foreign exchange only 4.6 percent.

....

What is the risk that my bank will fail and close its doors on me?

Currently about 8 out of every 1,000 commercial banks fail annually. That's under 1 percent.

....

What are the chances my newly published novel will be one of the ten best sellers of the year?

Don't buy that Malibu beach house just yet. Your chances of joining Stephen King, Judith Krantz, et al., are 10 in 4,877, and while that's a whole lot better than your chances of being struck by lightning, you might be interested to know that, stated another way, that gives you a chance of about one-fifth of one percent. Still, you beat the odds in getting your novel published in the first place, so keep on writing.

Risky Business

How likely am I to die without leaving a will?

Been putting that off, have you? You have plenty of company. Some 38 percent of those 45 to 54 don't have wills at the time of their deaths; 27 percent of those age 65 and over don't leave wills. Interestingly, older folks who are unmarried are less likely to die without a will than are married middle-aged people.

. . . .

Are men or women more likely to die without leaving a will?

Those "providers"—the men.

. . . .

What is the risk that my airline baggage will be lost, damaged, or delayed?

The last figures available show wide variability depending upon airline—ranging from nearly 12 pieces of luggage per thousand lost, damaged, or delayed by TWA to under 4 pieces per thousand similarly mishandled by Pan American.

. . . .

I want to go to medical school. What are my chances of getting in?

WHAT ARE THE CHANCES?

Getting better all the time. Your chances were only 34 percent in 1974. Today they are better than 55 percent. That's because applications dropped from more than 42,000 in 1974 to around 28,000 recently. Even applications to the prestigious Harvard Medical School have dropped from 4,200 in 1979 to 2,700 last year.

....

Am I more likely to do well on the SAT if I'm a boy or a girl?

Males do better on both the verbal and math portions of the test.

....

What are the chances I'll exceed a 600 score in either math or verbal portions of the SAT?

Not so good. About 7 to 8 percent exceed 600 in the verbal portion of the test, about 14 to 17 percent in the math portion.

....

If I don't finish high school, am I really more likely to be unemployed?

Afraid so. About twice as likely.

Risky Business

With all the publicity out there about the dangers of high cholesterol and fatty foods, I'm wondering just how risky it might be to go into the gourmet ice cream business?

Overall, not at all risky. The super-fatty gourmet types of ice cream are enjoying their greatest sales. Potato chip, candy, and croissant sales are also fat these days.

....

If I bring a malpractice suit against a hospital, what are my chances of winning?

High and getting better all the time. The win rate for those alleging "negligent surgical procedures" is now 58 percent, up from 38 percent just ten years ago. The chances of winning a "negligent treatment" or "negligent supervision" suit are also way up.

....

As a child under age 1, I'm wondering what the risk is that Mom will be away working a lot of the time.

51 percent.

....

As a woman, what are my chances of becoming a high-ranking corporate executive?

4.5 percent.

WHAT ARE THE CHANCES?

As a woman who holds down a full-time job outside the home, I'd like to know what the chances are that other family members will shoulder more responsibility for housework?

Nil. About all you can count on your spouse doing is running an electric can opener or popping something into the microwave oven.

....

As a professional man, how likely is it that my working wife will also be a professional?

42 percent.

....

What are the chances for my new business?

So-so. 50 percent of all new businesses go belly-up within five years.

....

How risky are franchise businesses?

Far less risky than business in general. The failure rate for franchises is only about 1 percent per year. Lucky 7-11.

Risky Business

As a woman, how likely am I to earn as much as a man?

Overall, women earn 70 percent of what men earn.

....

What are the chances I'll get a pension when I retire?

84 percent if you were earning over $2,000 per month; only 38 percent if you were earning under $500 per month.

....

Am I more likely to have access to a computer if I go to public school or private school?

Our computer tells us that your chances are quite a bit better in public school.

....

Will working during my pregnancy imperil my baby?

No, not under normal circumstances. In fact, *not* working seems to increase the risks. A study at the University of North Carolina indicates that women who work during pregnancy are only half as likely as their nonworking counterparts to have premature, low birth-weight babies.

What are the chances I'll still be working when I'm over 65 years of age?

15.8 percent of men and 7.3 percent of women over 65 are still in the labor force.

....

If we all live longer, aren't we going to end up with a disastrous surplus of unproductive people who will imperil our society?

Not according to a study commissioned by the National Academy of Sciences. When we all live longer in good health, this study found, America will actually be a *more* productive nation, with health-care, retirement-benefit, and Social Security costs reduced rather than increased.

....

How serious is the risk that I will end up in a job I find unsatisfactory?

Depends upon how much the job pays. Only 29 percent of those making more than $50,000 per year profess occupational dissatisfaction, while 48 percent of those making under $15,000 per year are dissatisfied.

....

What risk will be uppermost in my mind on my wedding night?

Risky Business

Sexual or romantic risks? No. 67 percent of all couples are most concerned about the financial risks of marriage—and, specifically, whether they will be able to afford one another the morning after.

....

Are there any hidden risks in having my spouse work?

You'll spend 37 percent less time talking with one another than do couples with just one wage-earner; you'll also spend 40 percent less time doing things together that you both consider fun.

....

Am I more likely to end up with a net worth of zero or a net worth in excess of $500,000?

The rags are more likely than the riches: 11 percent versus 2 percent.

....

Are housewives or career women more likely to have heart attacks?

Drop your apron and grab a briefcase. The risk of heart attack is almost twice as high for the housewife.

WHAT ARE THE CHANCES?

Are men who are employed or unemployed more likely to die of heart attacks?

Idle hands, bad heart. Being unemployed increases the risk of heart attack by 14 percent among males 25 to 64.

....

Are blue-collar or white-collar workers more likely to die next year?

Too much hard work apparently *will* kill you. Blue-collar laborers are 41 percent more likely than average to die next year. White-collar professionals are 28 percent less likely than average to chuck the good life next year.

....

Can I count on getting correct change at my local fast-food outlet?

Not as often as you can count on getting the wrong change, according to a Hudson Institute study that indicates that less than half the 21- to 25-year-olds working in these establishments make proper change for a two-item meal.

....

Is there much chance my car will be recalled because of some defect?

Risky Business

Yes. In fact, 60 percent of all automobiles sold in the 1980s were recalled for one defect or another. Many of these were minor.

....

Is it really possible to get rich by hard work—or do you have to inherit it?

82 percent of the "affluent" (people with net worths of $500,000 or more, exclusive of their homes) say they got rich by working hard; only 6 percent inherited wealth.

....

How much more likely am I to have an annual income in excess of $50,000 if I complete college as opposed to only the eighth grade?

Ten times more likely.

....

What's the chance I'll be a top executive of a major company if I didn't go to college?

Not too great, but not out of the question. 12 percent of top executives never went to college.

WHAT ARE THE CHANCES?

Am I more likely to become a top business executive if I start out as a laborer or as a lawyer?

Labor seems to provide better experience for leadership than does the law. About 10 percent of today's top execs climbed up from the bottom, where they began as "common laborers." Only 6 percent started out as lawyers.

....

Which states are most/least likely to boom in the coming years?

The U.S. Census Bureau has recently made some substantial changes in its year 2000 forecasts for several states. Florida is now expected to grow by two million fewer souls than previously forecast, Colorado by 800,000 less than was forecast five years ago, and Oregon by one million less. New York, on the other hand, which some were writing off as moribund, is now expected to grow by more than three million more than had been predicted, New Jersey by more than a million, Georgia by more than a million, Maryland by 700,000, and Massachusetts by 600,000.

....

What are the chances I'll grow up to be incompetent in writing and reading/in math?

22 percent of all adults are incompetent in writing and reading, and 33 percent are incompetent in math.

Risky Business

What are the chances I will complete four years of college?

19 percent.

....

Is an older or a newer house going to be riskier in terms of energy costs?

Oldies are not always goodies. On average, energy will cost you 35 percent more if you buy or rent a house built before 1940.

....

Is a business more likely to fail today than it was thirty years ago?

Yes. Twice as likely.

....

Is there any risk in wearing a necktie?

Yes, and you don't have to hang yourself with one to be at risk. Researchers at Cornell University conducted a study showing that 66 percent of all businessmen wear their ties too tight; 12 percent wear them so tight they actually diminish blood flow to the brain, diminishing cerebral function. It would be interesting to see how much a corporate-mandated loose-tie policy would up productivity and revenues, not to mention blood supply.

....

What are the chances I will have to commute one to two hours to work?

15 percent. 41 percent of us commute thirty minutes or less.

....

Are hospitals more likely to make mistakes in their favor or my favor when it comes to billing?

Check that bill carefully. Hospitals are three times more likely to make errors in their favor than in yours. When your bill is in excess of $10,000, overcharges are most common and average between $1,300 and $1,500. These most commonly relate to procedures that weren't actually performed, extra days in the hospital when you weren't actually there, or drugs and equipment you didn't actually use.

....

In which state will I earn the most/least money?

Connecticut and Alaska have the highest per capita incomes in the nation—more than double that of the state with the lowest per capita income: Mississippi.

Risky Business

Am I more likely to find work as an astronomer or an astrologer?

Judging by what's out there right now, it appears that there is considerably more demand for those who divine, rather than detect, the stars. There are 13,000 astrologers and only 3,000 astronomers.

....

Is it at all likely that one could work full-time and still be at the poverty level of income in the U.S.?

Yes. In fact, nearly 50 percent of those families defined as living in poverty have a family member who is working full-time.

....

Which sort of person is most likely to overpay for a new car: the person who shops around a lot, the person who distrusts dealers, or the "loyalist" who sticks with the same dealer car after car?

The person who distrusts dealers and hates the whole process of buying cars is, ironically, the one who, according to a California market research firm, will overpay. In fact, this person is three times more likely than any other to pay more than list price for a car. This person doesn't shop around, rushes into the buying process without any prior research, makes his purchase in haste and moves on. The careful shopper—the person who may spend a month or longer looking—is the least likely to overpay. The loyalists fall in the middle ground.

....

In terms of income, is it riskier going into biology or psychology?

Psychology—the pay, on average, will be about 40 percent less.

....

What are the chances I will finish high school if I give birth before I reach age 18?

Half what they would have been otherwise.

....

I know that it doesn't pay to become a schoolteacher, but is it just as financially risky becoming a public school administrator?

Not at all. In contrast with the low salaries of public school teachers, half of all public school administrators make at least $50,000 annually—which is more than what 80 percent of all other college graduates earn.

I'm suing the media for libel. What are my chances of winning?

Not good. A recent survey by the Libel Defense Resource Center reveals that three out of four libel cases get thrown out of court without trial. When the remaining cases do go to trial, plaintiffs such as yourself lose 80 percent of the time. Looking back over several years, moreover, it is clear that the trend is increasingly in favor of the media in these cases.

....

My daughter wants a formal wedding. What's the financial risk to me?

$13,310, if you're footing the entire bill. That's the average cost of a formal wedding, according to *Modern Bride* magazine.

....

I'm trying to decide whether I can afford marriage. What's the honeymoon going to cost me?

Average honeymoon expenditure in one recent survey was $2,127. You should think about the other expenditures, too. Newlyweds account for 50 percent of the china dinnerware and sterling silver flatware market; that 50 percent totals $418 million annually. Newlyweds also spend about $588 million on new furniture.

WHAT ARE THE CHANCES?

What are the chances I will die before my 25-year mortgage is paid off?

If you are a 30-year-old male, your chance of this happening is 1 in 9; if you are a 45-year-old male, the risk increases to 1 in 3. For the 30-year-old female, there is a lesser risk of 1 in 16, increasing to 1 in 5 for the 45-year-old female.

....

What are the chances I'm making less than $5 per hour?

1 in 3.

....

Does it cost society more to send a young person to a state pen or to Penn State?

It costs seven times more to send someone to a state pen.

....

Are the risks greater or less now than they were twenty years ago that as a retiree I will have to live below the poverty line?

Twenty years ago the risk of this was approaching 30 percent. Today it is under 13 percent.

Risky Business

What are the chances that when I'm retired I'll still have to pay state or federal income taxes?

50 percent.

....

Is it becoming riskier/less risky to be a woman—in terms of pay?

Definitely less risky. The pay gap, which remained at about 40 percent for decades, has now narrowed to a little under 30 percent overall and to less than 20 percent for women in their 20s.

....

If I'm a black teenager, am I at greater or lesser risk of dropping out of high school than I would have been ten years ago?

Considerably less risk. The black dropout rate has dropped from 27 percent a decade ago to 17 percent today. This is fast approaching the white dropout rate of 14 percent.

....

Which branch of the service has the highest desertion rate?

If you're planning (or perhaps, not planning) to make the military your career, your risk of becoming a deserter appears to be greatest in the Marine Corp, lowest in the Air Force.

WHAT ARE THE CHANCES?

I won't be retiring for another forty years. What are the chances there will still be money left in the Social Security system to pay my old-age benefits?

A recent analysis of the Social Security system indicates that you'll be able to collect. In fact, it looks like the system, even without any further modification, is going to be solvent for at least another sixty years.

....

Which cars are least risky from the standpoint of repairs?

Porsche is the most trouble-free, according to a recent survey of 75,000 auto owners. Mercedes-Benz came in second, with Toyota and Nissan in a tie for third. The only American cars to make the top-ten list were Cadillac, Buick, and Oldsmobile.

....

Isn't it true that most people who work for minimum wage are teenagers?

No, contrary to the assertion of some politicians, only 31 percent of those receiving minimum wage are in their teens; 21 percent are between 20 and 24, and 48 percent are 25 and up. Fully 63 percent of those earning minimum wage are women, many of whom are supporting children.

Risky Business

In school, do boys or girls get more attention from their teachers?

Boys—and this is true, according to a University of Iowa researcher, from kindergarten through college.

....

Will I make more money if I become a pharmacist or a jet pilot?

You'll fly financially higher in the jet. Pilots make, on average, $47,400. Chain-store pharmacists average $38,000.

....

Will I do better financially becoming a schoolteacher or a computer operator?

Ministering to real minds still pays better than operating the mechanical variety. The average schoolteacher makes $26,551, the average computer operator $19,100.

....

Are blue-collar or white-collar workers the ones most likely to be financially hurt during a recession?

White-collar workers, at least in the current economy, where a recessionary cheaper dollar boosts export-manufacturing orders and thus aids blue-collar workers.

WHAT ARE THE CHANCES?

How likely is it that if I am a senior at Yale I will graduate with honors?

Very high—about 50 percent, up from about 25 percent in 1968. This is attributed not to smarter Yalies but to the widespread phenomenon known as "grade inflation."

....

How likely am I to be late for work in Southern California in the year 2010?

Even more likely than you are now. Average freeway speed in Southern California is expected to decline from its present sluggish 35 mph to a truly slothful 19 mph by 2010.

....

If I want to become a school principal or superintendent, are my chances better if I'm a man or a woman, black or white?

A Department of Education study reveals that 95 percent of superintendents and 76 percent of principals are white males. "The phrase 'old boys club' has true meaning when it comes to the administration of our public schools," the study concluded.

....

Where is the office rental business the riskiest?

Houston and Dallas. Houston has an office vacancy rate of more than 30 percent, Dallas a vacancy rate of almost 30 percent. The empty offices of those two cities could accommodate all of the office workers in Atlanta. The two cities jointly have 82 million square feet of empty space.

....

Are the rich or the poor at greater risk of driving gas guzzlers?

The poor get fewer miles per gallon than the rich. In fact, fuel efficiency (miles per gallon in automobiles owned) and average family income are directly correlated. Those with incomes less than $10,000 per year get 13.9 mpg; those who make between $15,000 and $25,000 get 14.6 mpg; and those with incomes above $35,000 get 16.1 mpg and better.

....

Is a VCR (purchased for taping capability) a good investment risk, from the standpoint of actually getting used much?

Fewer and fewer people appear to be using their VCRs for taping. In 1988 only 24 percent of all VCR households taped a sport event in a typical week—down from 39 percent in 1985. Only 54 percent of these households taped a movie in a typical week in 1988—down from 70 percent in 1985. There are less expensive VCRs with only playback capability that may be a better investment.

WHAT ARE THE CHANCES?

Are some home improvements, in terms of return on money, riskier than others?

Definitely. If you're lucky, you may recoup half of what you put into a swimming pool. The typical new deck, on the other hand, will yield a 223 percent return on your investment. Other improvements that typically pay off include new paint, kitchen and bathroom remodeling, fireplaces, skylights, ceiling fans, new light fixtures, new entryways, and landscaping.

. . . .

Suit has been filed against me in federal court. What are the chances the court will actually hear the case and I will be tried?

48.9 percent.

. . . .

What are the chances my individual federal income tax return will be audited by the IRS?

Overall, the IRS audits 1.3 percent of all returns. The higher your income, however, the greater the chances of being audited. Only 0.4 percent of families with incomes under $10,000 are audited, while 3.5 percent of those with incomes over $50,000 are audited.

Risky Business

In which state is the risk of being audited by the IRS the greatest/least?

Greatest in the state of Washington, least in Maine. Maine taxpayers are about half as likely as other Americans to be audited. Westerners, who tend more often to be self-employed and involved in cash businesses, are, overall, the most likely to be audited.

In which states would I have to pay the most/the least state income taxes?

Most in New York and West Virginia, least in Connecticut, New Hampshire, and Tennessee, which have limited or no state income taxes.

Am I more likely to be audited by the IRS if I live in Las Vegas or Providence, Rhode Island?

You guessed it—Las Vegas. You're *five times* more likely to be audited in Las Vegas.

What about Chicago and Manhattan—where is an audit more likely?

Manhattanites are about 70 percent more likely to be audited than are Chicagoans.

....

Am I at greater risk of lying to the IRS about my income as I make more or less money each year?

In general, this risky practice increases with income. In fact, nearly 11 percent of all those who report income between $50,000 and $100,000 per year will try to conceal at least $1,000 of income from the IRS, whereas only about 3 percent of those making less than $25,000 per year do this. Those in the higher income bracket are more than six times more likely to try to conceal $10,000 or more of income than those in the $25,000 and under bracket.

....

What are the chances that if I am audited I will have to pay more than $1,000?

An IRS audit extracts $5,330 on average.

....

Am I more likely to be audited by the IRS if my business is held as a partnership, corporation, or sole proprietorship?

Risky Business

The IRS audited 2.4 percent of all corporate returns and 1.4 percent of all partnerships. But sole proprietorships with gross revenues of more than $100,000 were audited at a rate of 5.4 percent.

....

If I ask the IRS for advice on filling out my tax forms, what is the risk the information it provides will be wrong?

31 percent of all letter responses from the IRS contain serious errors, according to the General Accounting Office of the United States. Another 16 percent of these letter responses give unclear or incomplete answers. The risk of getting faulty information through the mail, then, is 41 percent. Telephone information is wrong, unclear, or incomplete 36 percent of the time.

....

Is it riskier to be a Catholic or a Jew if you are running for president of the United States?

Neither poses much risk anymore. In 1958, 25 percent of those polled said they would not vote for a Roman Catholic, 28 percent said they would not vote for a Jew. Today only 8 percent say they would not vote for a Catholic, and only 10 percent say they would not vote for a Jew. Having no religious convictions is far riskier for politicians. Fully 60 percent of those polled said they wouldn't vote for an atheist.

If I'm an openly avowed atheist, what are my chances at occupying the Oval Office?

A tad better than if you are openly homosexual. 31 percent of the electorate say they would not rule out voting for you just because you don't believe in God.

....

If I'm openly gay, what are the chances I can be elected president of the United States?

At present, only 26 percent of the electorate say they would consider voting for a homosexual running for the presidency.

....

What are the chances a bill introduced into the U.S. Congress will actually pass?

Less than 8 percent.

....

What are the chances Congress will override a presidential veto?

Only about 4 percent.

Risky Business

What are the chances my son will become a doctor/lawyer/ nurse?

For every 100,000 boys, 567 will become doctors, 1,170 will become lawyers, 150 will become nurses.

....

What are the chances my daughter will become a doctor/ lawyer/nurse?

For every 100,000 girls, 223 will become doctors, 682 will become lawyers, and 17,475 will become nurses.

....

What are the chances my little tiger will grow up to be a pro football player?

About .0001 percent (12 out of every 100,000 boys, to be precise).

....

What are the chances my little Einstein will grow up to get a Ph.D.?

Eight out of every 1,000 children will get a Ph.D. Now you know why pro football players make so much more than professors.

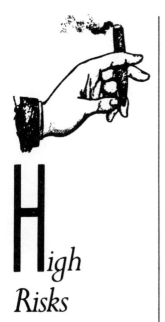

8

Higher Risks

Smoking, Drugs, Alcohol

What are the chances I will be able to stop smoking with the help of hypnosis?

Look deeply into our eyes and believe us when we tell you that figures provided by the Smoking Cessation Research Institute indicate that your chances of quitting are actually better using willpower alone (about 1 in 4 compared to 1 in 5 using hypnosis).

Am I more or less likely to smoke as I get older?

The older you are, the less likely you will smoke. Some 32 percent of those 20 to 34 smoke, 31.5 percent of those 35 to 44 smoke, 29.9 percent of those 44 to 64 smoke, and only 13.5 of those 65 and older smoke.

....

Am I more or less likely to smoke if I am divorced?

Let's clear the air on this burning question: the divorced are a breathtaking 56 percent more likely to smoke than are married folks. Freud could no doubt make something of this.

....

Are men or women at greater risk of becoming smokers?

Smoking is apparently still the "manly" thing to do. Males are 15.6 percent more likely to smoke than females.

....

What are the chances I will be able to quit smoking without some sort of help?

About 25 percent. Males, light smokers, and those facing serious illness are the most likely to be able to quit on their own.

....

Which is more dangerous, smoking a regular cigarette or a marijuana cigarette?

I terms of exposure to carbon monoxide (linked to coronary artery disease), smoking one marijuana cigarette is, typically, the equivalent of smoking five tobacco cigarettes. In terms of exposure to tar (linked to cancer), smoking one joint is equivalent, on average, to smoking three tobacco cigarettes. A UCLA School of Medicine study has found that those who smoke just three or four joints a day suffer as much respiratory damage as those who smoke a whole pack of tobacco cigarettes a day. Water pipes, incidentally, have been found to be ineffective filters for either tar or carbon monoxide.

....

Does marijuana use increase the risk of any major mental illness?

In a fifteen-year study of more than 45,000 Swedish soldiers, researchers at the Karolinska Institute found that those who have used marijuana more than 50 times are 6 times more likely than nonusers to develop schizophrenia. They found a consistent, direct correlation between the amount of marijuana use and the incidence of schizophrenia. Those who had used marijuana 11 to 50 times had a three-fold increase in their risk of developing schizophrenia. The Swedish researchers do not think that marijuana itself causes schizophrenia but that it may help trigger it in those otherwise predisposed by other factors.

....

As a reader of *Ladies' Home Journal,* how likely am I to have used marijuana or cocaine?

According to the *Journal* itself, 28 percent of its readers have used marijuana, 9 percent have enlivened their reading material with cocaine.

....

What is the probability a young person 12 to 17 used marijuana/alcohol last month?

12 percent for marijuana, 31 percent for alcohol.

....

What is the risk my fourth-grader will experiment with marijuana?

25 percent.

....

What are the chances my high school senior will get drunk this week?

50 percent.

....

Won't letting a child use drugs or alcohol early in life reduce the risk that he/she will go on to abuse those substances later in life?

No. The earlier a child begins using drugs/alcohol the more likely he/she will have health problems and expanded substance dependence later in life.

....

Is my child more likely to recognize that alcohol or marijuana is a drug?

A recent survey reveals that only 42 percent of all fourth-graders know that alcohol is a drug, while 81 percent recognize marijuana as a drug.

....

Are girls or boys more likely to experiment with a variety of drugs?

Girls.

....

What are the chances that when I commit a crime I will be high on drugs or alcohol?

About 50 percent.

....

Are Vietnam vets at increased risk of requiring hospitalization for drug/alcohol abuse?

Yes—their risk is increased four-fold for alcohol abuse, five-fold for drug abuse.

....

What are the chances I will grow up to be a heavy drinker, a teetotaler?

8 percent of all adults are heavy drinkers, while 35 percent abstain entirely.

....

What is America's number-one drug problem among youth—alcohol, cocaine, marijuana, or heroin?

Alcohol.

....

Are married men or divorced men/bachelors at higher risk of being heavy drinkers?

It appears that marriage, contrary to what some would have us believe, really is a refuge from and not an invitation to take to the bottle. Some 66 percent of all married men are either abstainers or light drinkers; only 34 percent are heavy drinkers. For the bachelors and the divorced men, just the opposite is true: 66 percent are heavy drinkers, 34 percent abstainers/light drinkers.

If I'm an alcoholic, how likely is it that I will be able to get off the sauce and *stay* off?

Fewer than 10 percent of all alcoholics are able to abstain entirely from alcohol for as long as four years.

....

My ten-year-old appears to be drunk every once in a while. Is this at all likely?

Yes. The National Council on Alcoholism reports that 100,000 ten- and eleven-year-olds get drunk at least once a week.

....

My parents are alcoholic. Does this increase my risk of becoming an alcoholic myself?

Yes. You have a four times greater risk of becoming alcoholic than do the children of nonalcoholics.

....

If I'm the son of an alcoholic but am adopted by nondrinkers, am I still more likely than average to become an alcoholic myself?

Yes. You are still four times more likely than average to become an alcoholic yourself.

....

Is a home in which parents abstain entirely from alcohol the least likely to produce adolescents who drink heavily?

No. There is mounting evidence that a totally negative attitude toward alcohol can do as much to encourage adolescent drinking as a totally permissive or uncaring attitude.

....

Is there any link between television and alcoholism?

No one knows for sure, but it has been calculated that the average child will see booze consumed on TV an average of 75,000 times before he/she reaches legal drinking age.

....

Are women in their childbearing years more or less likely to use drugs and/or alcohol?

More likely. 72 percent more likely to use marijuana, 144 percent more likely to use heroin, 61 percent more likely to use cocaine, 61 percent more likely to use alcohol regularly— more likely in each instance than the general population.

What are the chances that if I'm involved in a serious swimming, boating, or snowmobile accident I've been boozing heavily?

Pretty high: 30 to 50 percent.

....

Would placing higher taxes on beer reduce the risk of automobile fatalities among young people?

The National Council on Alcoholism states that increasing federal excise tax on beer, the alcoholic beverage of choice among young people, would reduce consumption and could cut alcohol-related motor vehicle fatalities by as much as 45 to 50 percent for 18- to 20-year-old men and women. Alcohol-related highway deaths are the leading cause of death among 15- to 24-year-olds.

....

Is alcohol more dangerous for men or women?

Alcohol is more toxic to women than to men. Alcohol becomes more concentrated in the blood of women than in the blood of men because males have more body water to dilute the alcohol. Thus it takes far less alcohol to inflict serious liver and brain damage in women.

WHAT ARE THE CHANCES?

Am I more likely to be an alcoholic if I'm a Baptist or an Orthodox Jew?

Baptist. Orthodox Jews are almost never alcoholics.

....

Who is most likely to have to be hospitalized for alcohol/ drug abuse, blacks or whites?

Blacks are about 35 percent more likely than whites to be hospitalized for alcoholism and about twice as likely to be hospitalized for drug abuse.

....

Am I more likely to be hospitalized for alcohol abuse or drug abuse?

Overall, Americans are four times more likely to be hospitalized for alcohol abuse than for drug abuse.

....

What is the risk my too-young-to-drive teenager will ride in a car next month driven by somebody on drugs or alcohol?

38 percent.

High Risks

Where am I at greatest risk of falling in with beer guzzlers?

Head for New Hampshire, which has the highest annual per capita consumption of beer in the nation: 51.31 gallons per each adult.

....

Where am I at greatest risk of being exposed to serious drinkers?

If by serious drinkers you mean those who consume distilled spirits—remain in New Hampshire.

....

Where am I at greatest risk of rubbing shoulders with wine bibbers?

Pad your shoulders in Nevada, the wine-bibbing capital of the nation. California is runner-up for the red and the white.

....

Am I at greater risk of abusing tranquilizers if I'm a woman or a man?

Woman—simply because women far more frequently than men use tranquilizers.

What is the chance that a child 12 to 17 used cocaine last month? Ever?

1.8 percent last month, 5.2 percent ever.

....

What is the chance that someone 18 to 25 used cocaine last month? Ever?

7.7 percent last month and 25.2 percent ever.

....

What is the chance that someone 25 or over used cocaine last month? Ever?

2.1 percent last month, 9.5 percent ever.

....

Does cocaine use during pregnancy increase the chances of subsequent crib death?

Yes—by 50 times.

....

In which region of the country is cocaine use most prevalent?

The West. 5.2 percent of Westerners are current cocaine users compared with 2.5 percent in the Northeast, 2.6 percent in the North-Central, and 1.4 percent in the South.

9

Fat Chance

Food, Diet, Weight

In which country of the world are people at the highest risk of being obese?

In the United States.

Am I at greater risk of being fat if I'm a man or a woman?

According to a nationwide Louis Harris poll, 66 percent of the men were overweight, compared with 63 percent of the women.

Are men or women most likely to acknowledge a weight problem?

Women are more likely than men to consider themselves overweight, even though men are actually just as likely to have weight problems. 59 percent of women surveyed think they weigh too much, while only 37 percent of the men do.

....

Are the rich or poor more likely to be overweight?

The poor. The Duchess of Windsor once said you can never be too rich or too thin. There does seem to be a relationship between the two.

....

What is the risk that, as a teenager, I will be dissatisfied with my weight and will either be dieting or trying to build myself up?

Nearly 60 percent.

....

If I quit smoking, is there really a risk that I'll gain weight?

Yes. People who stop smoking gain, on average, eight pounds. Females tend to gain more than males.

....

As a woman, by how much will I increase my desirability among men if I become decidedly thin?

Probably not at all. Even though a recent Gallup Poll shows that most women think men desire a truly thin woman, the same poll indicates that men actually want a more average body type in their mates. Only 18 percent of the poll's male respondents said they desired a thin woman as opposed to one of average build. Average is 5'3⅓" and 134 pounds (dress sizes 10–12).

....

Are males or females more likely to be bulimic (binge eaters who then induce vomiting)?

Females—up to five percent. Males—less than one percent.

....

I'm a woman with a weight problem. If I cut out drinking, how much faster can I expect to lose weight?

Not at all faster. Researchers at the Centers for Disease Control and at Johns Hopkins University have reported recently that, compared with nondrinkers, women who consume alcohol 7 to 13 times per week consistently lose more weight—just the opposite of what everyone had thought. These conclusions are based on two massive national food-intake surveys, and the association between alcohol consumption and reduced body weight was found to be substantial.

WHAT ARE THE CHANCES?

Does being an overweight male MBA put me at any particular financial risk?

Odd you should ask. It was just the other day that we were observing that, according to a study from the University of Pittsburgh, the overweight male MBA earns $4,000 a year less than his lean male counterpart. We haven't heard yet what financial fate awaits the overweight female MBA.

....

Are *Ladies' Home Journal* readers more likely to become addicted to dieting, compulsive overeating, or sex?

They are at highest risk, according to a *Journal* survey, of being compulsive overeaters (20 percent). Fewer are addicted to dieting (8 percent) and fewer still to sex (4 percent).

....

Does my risk of eating out at fast-food restaurants increase or decrease with age?

Your exposure to the greasy kid stuff decreases steadily with age. Those between 18 and 24 have a 71 percent likelihood of chowing down at a fast-food outlet this week, whereas those between 35 and 49 have a 53 percent chance and those golden-agers (65 +) have only a 26 percent chance of passing through the Golden Arches (and similar) this week.

By how much will the use of artificial sweeteners help me lose weight?

By zero. In fact, according to an American Cancer Society study of 79,000 women, those who use artificial sweeteners are actually more prone to weight gain than are nonusers. This held true despite the initial weight or types of food eaten.

....

I like to please my dinner guests. Which meats, in terms of consumer acceptance, are the least liked?

Dinner invitations from you will be considered a definite culinary risk if you are in the habit of serving liverwurst, venison, or gizzards of any description.

....

Is it risky to stop drinking milk as we get older?

Those who don't drink milk have three times the risk of getting colorectal cancer than do those who drink a couple glasses of milk daily.

....

I've heard that on the typical American diet each of us eats a *ton* of fat in our lifetimes. Is that possible?

WHAT ARE THE CHANCES?

The typical American diet actually puts the average individual at risk of consuming, over a lifetime, 5,000 to 7,000 pounds of pure fat.

....

What is the chance I will consume a dozen or more pounds of cheese in a single year?

If you are an average American, the chance is 100 percent. The typical American currently eats 26 pounds of cheese per year, 65 to 75 percent of which is fat.

....

I love chocolate, but I just nibble at it. Is there a chance I'm eating too much?

Considering its high fat content and considering the fact that the average American now eats ten pounds of chocolates per year, yes, there is some risk. Americans now spend $4.8 *billion* on chocolates each year.

....

In terms of the cholesterol risk, which single food contributes more of this stuff to the typical American diet than any other?

Eggs contribute 35.88 percent of all cholesterol consumed by Americans. Beef (steaks and roasts) come in a distant second, contributing 8.69 percent. Fried fish, by comparison, provides only a little over one half of one percent. Yogurt provides a trifling .08 percent.

....

Which foods commonly consumed by Americans contain the most fat?

Hamburgers, cheeseburgers, meat loaf, hot dogs, ham, and lunch meat. Fish, among the meats, contributes the least fat.

....

What factors would put me at risk of becoming a bagel-eater?

The most common bagel-eater is a college-educated Northeasterner between the ages of 35 and 44 with a household income in excess of $40,000. Maybe more of us should eat bagels already.

....

Is there any chance that if I ate Frosted Flakes as a child I'll still be eating them as an adult?

Flaky eating habits apparently die hard. The chances are 50 percent.

10

Elements of Risk

Weather, Pollution, Natural and Unnatural Disasters

....

What are the chances that a devastating earthquake will hit Southern California within the next twenty-five years?

50 percent—and the experts say that such a quake, measuring 8.0 or more on the Richter scale, will kill 3,000 to 14,000 people, seriously injure up to 52,000 people, and will cause about $17 billion in property damage.

....

What are the chances that a huge earthquake will hit the San Francisco Bay Area within the next twenty-five years?

50 percent—at an estimated cost in lives of 3,000 to 11,000 and

an estimated cost in property damage of $38 billion. Serious injuries could total 44,000.

....

I hate rain. Where is the risk of the wet stuff lowest?

You might try Antarctica. There are spots there where it has not rained for at least 100 years.

....

Is it more likely to rain on any given day in Juneau, Alaska, or Seattle?

Juneau—where it rains 60 percent of the time (220 days out of the year). Seattle drizzles 43 percent of the time—157 days out of the year.

....

Where is the risk of exposure to ozone air pollution the greatest?

The risks are greatest, in descending order, in Los Angeles, San Diego, Houston, New York City, various areas of Connecticut, Providence, R.I., Sacramento, Philadelphia, Atlantic City, and Chicago. Los Angeles is far and away the worst, with an average 154 days each year during which ozone levels exceed Environmental Protection Agency limits. Second-worst San Diego exceeds limits on an average 11 days.

....

Is Houston at risk of sinking out of sight?

If subsidence continues in Houston at its present rate, yes. This subsidence—caused primarily by pumping water from the aquifer under the city—is proceeding at a rate sufficient to make even a 45-story building sink from sight by the year 2180. As the ground subsides, the Gulf moves in. Pumping water from aquifer has caused Mexico City to sink 35 feet in the past seventy years; California's San Joaquin Valley has dropped 30 feet due to pumping for irrigation. Subsidence is a major problem throughout the Southwest. Water levels have dropped so far in some areas that it's no longer cost-effective to pump it to the surface.

....

How much of the world's land surface is presently threatened with desertification—extreme aridity caused by dropping water tables?

Perhaps as much as 35 percent of the planet's surface faces this life-threatening peril. 850 million people presently live in these areas.

If we take immediate measures, can we quickly eliminate the atmospheric ozone hole that scientists say poses a serious peril to human health?

No. The "hole" will persist for at least 100 years even if we immediately cut by 90 percent emissions of ozone-destroying chemicals. If we delay such cuts by even 10 years, however, the hole will persist fifty years longer, according to atmospheric science experts at Harvard and elsewhere. So far the major industrialized nations have agreed only to measures that would cut these emissions by 30 percent in 1994 and by 50 percent in 1999.

....

Which states have the most/least hazardous waste sites on the Environmental Protection Agency's priority list, indicating need for immediate cleanup?

New Jersey heads the list, followed by New York, Pennsylvania, Michigan, and California. Alaska, Hawaii, and Nevada have no priority sites.

....

What's the chance the next bridge I cross is not all that it's cracked up to be?

Cracked may be the right word. A recent study by the Federal Highway Administration disclosed that 42 percent of the highway bridges in this country have deficiencies that limit their load, serviceability, or safety.

....

Given the conservation consciousness of the last few decades, are we still at risk of running short of good water?

More so than ever. In 1950 the U.S. was using 180 billion gallons of water a day. Now we use 450 billion gallons a day, a 2.5-fold increase in just three decades, according to the U.S. Geological Survey. Both water quantity and water quality are declining. Many urban areas are having to buy water from increasingly distant sources at increasingly higher costs. Agriculture uses most of our water. It presently takes 1.5 million gallons of water to produce the food eaten by just one person each year.

....

What percentage of our nation's lakes and streams are suffering overuse, making them vulnerable to pollution and depletion?

An estimated 68 percent.

....

What are the chances that the water my family and I are drinking is contaminated?

20 percent of all water systems are contaminated by chemicals, many of them toxic.

....

We used to hear a lot about the "population bomb." Has the risk of world overpopulation gone away?

Unfortunately, no. It took hundreds of thousands of years for the human population to reach 1 billion in the year 1800. The next billion materialized in just 130 years (1930). The third billion took a mere 30 more years to produce (1960). Now, in less than two decades, world population has soared to more than 5 billion, and, by 1997, there will be more than 6 billion humans alive on the planet.

The world population is currently growing by more than 90 million people a year. A decade ago it was considerably less—75 million. World population is actually growing even a little faster than some of the so-called "alarmists" warned it would twenty years ago. New food-production technologies, meanwhile, have not been able to keep up with the exploding population, with the result that more than half a billion people are now without even minimally adequate nourishment.

....

In terms of health hazards, is it riskier to live in a modern, well-insulated building or in a drafty old one?

Riskier to live in the modern building, according to a number of studies. One of these compared 400,000 Army trainees, some of whom live in new modern barracks and some of whom live in old barracks. The trainees housed in the new energy-efficient barracks had 50 percent more respiratory infections than those living in the old buildings. The fresh air that gets into the old buildings apparently provides a healthier environment.

....

How likely is it that the new office building I'm working in has the "sick building syndrome"?

According to the World Health Organization, up to 30 percent of all new and remodeled office buildings cause health problems.

Head Games

Emotions, Stress, Self-Esteem, Mind, Spirit

11

What are the chances that as an adult I will lose my faith in organized religion?

38 percent.

Will having a room of my own as a teenager increase or decrease my risk of mental illness later in life?

Decrease it.

What are the chances I'll have a supernatural experience?

About 1 in 17, according to one survey. And the joke is that if you live in California your chances are more like 1 in 3.

WHAT ARE THE CHANCES?

What are the chances I'll be a fingernail-biter?

About 1 in 6 overall. More horrifying yet: fully 33 percent of America's more than 40 million fingernail biters are also toenail biters! While 16.6 percent of the general population regularly bites its nails, 25 percent of all Army recruits and 40 percent of all children/teenagers do so.

....

Do do-gooders have better immunity than Scrooges?

Yes, according to preliminary studies at Harvard and elsewhere that suggest that altruism boosts immune response.

....

Will doing regular volunteer work diminish any significant health risks?

In an ambitious University of Michigan Survey Research Center study of 2,700 people, researchers found that, for men, doing volunteer work could increase life expectancy. There was a 2.25 times greater incidence of death among men (during the study period) who did no volunteer work, compared with men who volunteered at least once a week. Such dramatic differences were not noted for women—perhaps, the researchers surmised, because women are already involved in caring for others, typically their families.

Head Games

Are poor listeners at higher risk of getting sick?

Yes, according to a University of Maryland study that found that those who like to talk as much as possible and listen as little as possible are at increased risk of developing high blood pressure.

....

Do I risk being regarded as an oddball if I believe in astrology?

Nancy Reagan and you have plenty of company. According to a national Roper Organization poll, 23 percent of all Americans state outright that they believe in astrology. Another 30 percent indicate they might have some belief in it but "weren't sure." Less than half of all Americans state flatly they don't believe in it. Almost 40 percent, to the chagrin of the scientific community, say they think astrology is either "very scientific" or "sort of scientific."

....

Will people think I'm crazy if I tell them I believe in witches and ghosts?

Maybe not crazy, but many will no doubt think you are a bit odd. Still, 11 percent of the population shares your belief in these supernatural entities, according to a Gallup poll.

Am I more likely to be truthful with a computer or a psychologist?

You're more likely to truthfully answer questions put to you by a computer than by a psychologist, according to a Duke University study.

....

Does brief separation from parents of very young children pose any health risk to the children?

Some researchers believe that even day-care separation for children under six months old can pose risk, increasing susceptibility to various diseases later in life. Various studies show that separations, especially those caused by divorce, hospitalization, or death of a parent, can result in immune abnormalities in children.

....

If I get into an argument with my parents, what are the chances I will win?

Not so good. Parents prevail almost 90 percent of the time. It's called survival of the largest.

....

What are the chances that, as a college student, I will frequently or occasionally cheat on a test?

30.4 percent. Up from 20.6 percent in 1966.

....

Does anxiety increase a woman's risk of having premenstrual syndrome (PMS)?

Yes. One survey revealed that 41 percent of "very anxious" women have PMS while only 21 percent of "calm" women do.

....

Does a full moon really increase the risk of "madness" or other unusual behavior?

An analysis of forty studies related to this issue indicates there is no correlation between moon phases and human behavior. So, if your neighbor howls at the moon, he's perfectly healthy.

....

What are some of the major risk factors for mental and emotional problems faced by young children?

Researchers at George Washington University Medical School note that infants exposed to the following risks are more likely than others to have emotional problems and reduced mental ability, as measured by IQ: absent father, mother who suffers from mental illness at least twice in her lifetime, nonspontaneous mother who seldom smiles at or touches infant, highly anxious mother, head of household who is unemployed or unskilled, four or more older children in family.

The researchers found that when none of these risks was present, the average IQ of the child was 118. IQ was found to decline steadily with the number of risks present. Other researchers confirm that factors such as these play crucial roles, especially in infants from birth to three years old. What happens during this period, these researchers believe, has a large impact on mental/emotional health and criminality in later life.

....

As a woman, what mental health problem is most likely to afflict me?

A phobia or irrational fear of something. Many phobias are characterized by panic attacks.

....

Does watching a lot of television pose any risk to my child?

Pediatric studies link childhood obesity with TV watching. Others worry that constant TV watching may diminish respect for human life. Between the ages of 5 and 15 the average

American child, according to another study, sees more than 13,400 people killed on television.

....

Where am I most likely/least likely to find born-again Christians?

Most likely in the South, where 50 percent profess to being "born again," least likely in the Northwest, where only 17 percent make this claim.

....

What are the chances the next person I meet will be a born-again Christian?

33 percent.

....

Is there a chance I'll never be satisfied with life?

Yes, but that risk declines steadily with age. Whereas most people fear growing older, satisfaction with life actually increases in direct relationship with age. According to pollster Louis Harris, only 53 percent of us profess to be satisfied with life when we are 18 to 24; that figure rises to 59 percent among those 25 to 34, to 62 percent among those 35 to 39, and to 72 percent among those 50 and older.

WHAT ARE THE CHANCES?

Are people who mistrust others more likely to be untrustworthy themselves?

Yes. According to a number of studies, people who tend to be suspicious of others are themselves more likely to be cheaters, liars, manipulators.

. . . .

Are trustful people more likely to enjoy good mental/emotional health than the mistrustful?

Yes. A variety of studies show that trustful people, far from being the gullible, naive types who are victimized by others, are actually the kind of people others most frequently seek out as friends. They are far better liked and have far fewer mental/emotional problems.

. . . .

Are trustful or mistrustful people likely to live longer?

A fifteen-year study at Duke University makes it clear that trustful individuals are significantly less prone to premature death than mistrustful people.

. . . .

In terms of self-esteem and intelligence, is the "only child" at a disadvantage compared with children who have siblings?

No. Studies indicate that "onlies" usually have *higher* self-esteem than do children with siblings. Other studies indicate that "onlies" have higher IQs than do children who have many siblings.

....

Does a free display of emotion reduce health risks in men?

That's been the theory for some time. Now a study at Johns Hopkins University School of Medicine seems to confirm it. This long-range study indicates that the free emoter—the man who lets it "all hang out"—is 16 times less likely to get cancer than are loner types who keep it all bottled up inside. This is true despite the fact that the free emoters are the types most of us would think of as more unstable than the other types; the free emoters are subject to open bouts of anxiety, depression, "acting out," and seem to be more easily upset. In reality, it seems the other types, including those who express positive, upbeat attitudes, are merely concealing their anguish—to their detriment. The sunny, always optimistic types have a cancer rate in between the open emoters and the cold loners.

....

Will I be regarded as a kook if I tell people I believe UFOs are real and not imaginary?

Several national surveys have shown that more than half of all Americans believe UFOs are real objects that could conceivably come from other worlds. Some 10 percent of all Americans say they have personally seen UFOs.

....

If I tell people I really believe in lucky numbers, will they look at me cross-eyed?

That's a risk you won't have to face at least 43 percent of the time. That's the percentage of your fellow Americans who also firmly believe in lucky numbers. 12 percent of the population also admits to a firm belief in lucky charms—which they carry with them whenever possible.

....

Does living with somebody reduce the risk of death?

Depends on whether you're male or female. Having company apparently agrees with males, but not with females. Women who live in a household with other people are 2 percent more likely to die next year than are women who live alone. Males living with others have 14.3 percent less chance of dying next year.

....

Does "networking" reduce health risks?

Apparently. A University of California, Berkeley, study of 5,000 people indicates that a rich social life significantly prolongs life. Those with a network of friends, relatives, and links with community organizations were two times less likely to die during the study period than those who lived in isolation.

....

Is a gas-station attendant or a business executive at higher risk of heart attack due to psychological job stress?

The gas-station attendant. A study of nearly 5,000 men has shown that such supposedly low-responsibility, low-stress jobs as cashier, cook, gas-station attendant, and assembly line worker are actually much more stressful than far higher-paying jobs that require advanced training. The critical difference has to do with control. Those who have little control over their work were found to be two to four times more likely to have heart attacks than were those who have a lot of responsibilities (such as professionals and executives) but who have a great deal of control over their own work.

....

I feel that scientists are actually dangerous. Does this make me peculiar, or do I have company?

You have company. 53 percent believe scientists are dangerous people. The scientists, of course, still think you're peculiar—even if you do have plenty of company.

WHAT ARE THE CHANCES?

What are the chances I will win a Medal of Honor if I serve in the military during a major war?

The chances of war making you a recognized hero have varied very little from World War I through the Vietnam War. They are, overall, 2.6 in 10 million—remarkably similar to your chances of being killed by a poisonous snake.

....

If I take a polygraph test and lie, what is the risk I will be detected?

According to some studies, there's about a 72 percent chance you will be collared by the machine.

....

What is the risk that if I take a polygraph test it will incorrectly say that I lied?

At least 1 in 15 will thus be falsely fingered by the mechanical Big Brother.

....

What factors will put me at risk of being perceived as boring?

The characteristics of the boring person, according to researchers at North Carolina University, are a penchant for complaining about themselves, frequently asking pointless, dead-end questions, showing little interest in others, and indulging in small talk.

....

How likely am I to change my plans because of an astrological forecast?

7 percent. (Higher if you're Nancy Reagan.)

....

Am I more likely to visit a shrink if I live in New York or California?

New York. Northeasterners, in general, are more than 50 percent more likely to consult psychiatrists than Westerners. Southerners are the least likely to call the head doctor.

....

Is a 30-year-old or a 50-year-old more likely to consult a psychiatrist?

Those 25 to 44 are 50 percent more likely to consult psychiatrists than those 45 to 64.

WHAT ARE THE CHANCES?

Are males or females more likely to consult psychiatrists?

Females are 37 percent more likely.

. . . .

Are male or female adults more likely to be admitted to a hospital for psychiatric care?

Males are 42.5 percent more likely to be hospitalized for mental/emotional problems.

. . . .

Are male or female children at greater risk of requiring psychiatric hospitalization?

9 percent higher for the male child.

. . . .

What is the risk I will be admitted to a hospital for psychiatric care next year?

The chance is 550 in 100,000 if you are white, 932 in 100,000 if you are black, 19 in 100,000 if you are an Alaskan native.

. . . .

If I am hospitalized for psychiatric care, is it more likely I will go voluntarily or be committed?

Contrary to the impression many soap operas still give, most (71 percent) go voluntarily.

....

In which area of the country am I at greatest risk of having to be hospitalized for psychiatric care, and at least risk?

Not surprisingly, the crime and stress capital of the nation—Washington, D.C.—has the highest rate of admissions for psychiatric care (a rate that is nearly double that of its nearest "competitor," Georgia, and nearly 6 times that of the states in which one is least likely to require psychiatric hospitalization—Montana and Hawaii).

....

Does simply being in the military increase the risk of being admitted to a hospital for psychiatric care?

Yes. It almost doubles that risk.

....

Are Vietnam veterans more likely to require psychiatric hospitalization than nonvets?

Vietnam vets are 2.5 times more likely to require psychiatric hospitalization.

WHAT ARE THE CHANCES?

As a Vietnam vet, I'm wondering, what is my risk of suffering posttraumatic stress disorder?

1 in 7 Vietnam vets suffer from this disorder, which is often characterized by vivid "reliving" of war events.

....

Was it riskier serving in Vietnam or in the military outside of Vietnam during the Vietnam war—in terms of subsequent adverse health events?

Much riskier serving in Vietnam—about twice as risky in terms of a broad spectrum of health variables ranging from depression, alcohol abuse, anxiety, hearing loss, and low sperm counts.

....

Was it riskier to be an American soldier in Vietnam or a veteran of that war?

In a sense, there was more risk once the war was *over*. A shocking 100,000 Vietnam veterans—twice the number killed in action—have taken their own lives since the war ended.

....

Who is at the greatest risk of committing suicide?

Men in their 20s and 30s whose wives die.

....

Are the married or the unmarried more likely to kill themselves?

People who *never* marry are as unlikely to commit suicide as are the happily married. The divorced and those whose spouses die are at higher risk.

....

Am I really more likely to kill myself on or near a major holiday?

Recent studies suggest that the link between holidays and suicide is a myth—with one exception: New Year's Day. Apparently many people think New Year's Day is the appropriate time to act on their final resolution. Overall, however, holidays are actually a period of considerably fewer suicides.

....

Are American blacks or whites more likely to kill themselves?

Whites are more than twice as likely to commit suicide than blacks in this country.

WHAT ARE THE CHANCES?

In terms of contributing to the development of stress-induced major illness, which of the following "life events" are the riskiest: divorce or marriage? Marriage or the death of a close family member? Pregnancy or foreclosure on a mortgage? Major personal injury or detention in jail? Christmas or a ticket for disturbing the peace? Making a major change in your eating habits or in your social activities?

Divorce is substantially riskier than marriage; marriage is a bit less risky than death of a close family member; pregnancy is quite a bit riskier than a mortgage foreclosure; detention in jail is moderately more risky than a major personal injury; Christmas is slightly more perilous than getting a ticket for disturbing the peace; making a major change in your social activities is a little more dangerous than changing your eating habits.

....

What stressful life event most predisposes a person to a major illness?

Death of a spouse—followed, at some distance, by divorce and, in third place, marital separation.

12

Sporting Chance

Sports/Gambling

How risky is professional grand prix race-car driving?

One recent study indicates that the possibility of accidental death for the racer is a least 16.8 times greater than for the average white male.

....

Is it riskier being an active thoroughbred racehorse or a retired one?

Retirement may prove more hazardous to horse health. Some former racers become pampered pets, but more, the experts say, are turned into pet food.

....

WHAT ARE THE CHANCES?

Are my chances of becoming a Division I college football player greater if I'm from Texas or California?

Texas produces more Division I college football players than any other state—more than 14 percent. Florida produces the second most.

....

I'm a female high school student who loves to participate in high school sports. Where am I most likely/least likely to have this opportunity?

Most likely in Iowa and South Dakota, least likely in the South, especially in South Carolina and Florida.

....

What are the chances a high school athlete will compete in college as well?

50 percent.

....

What are the chances that if I become a National Football League player I'll earn more than $200,000?

Start looking for a tax shelter. Some 36 percent of NFL players are making more than $200,000. A few years ago only 5 percent were making that much.

Sporting Chance

Outside of quarterback, which is the most financially rewarding position on a professional football team? Least financially rewarding?

Defensive linemen are the next most highly compensated; punters get the least.

....

What are the chances an offensive lineman will play four or more years in the NFL?

Less than 50 percent.

....

As a college athlete, what are the chances I'll get drafted by the pros?

Only 8 percent of college baseball, basketball, and football players get drafted by the pros. And only 2 percent of those drafted actually make the pros.

....

What are the chances my career as a professional football or basketball player will be a long one?

Not good. Less than half the players who initially make pro football or basketball teams last even four years.

WHAT ARE THE CHANCES?

What are the chances that as a professional football player I'll have a disabling injury?

You can count on it. Virtually 100 percent of all pro football players eventually suffer an injury sufficient to cause some or complete loss of career.

....

What are the chances that, as a major league baseball manager, I'll still have my job at the beginning of the next season?

56 percent.

....

As manager of the New York Yankees, what are the chances I'll still have this job next season?

During the Steinbrenner regime, 0 percent.

....

As an NFL head coach, what are the chances I'll still be in my job at the beginning of next season?

81 percent.

....

As a National Hockey League head coach, what are the chances I'll still have my job at the beginning of the next season?

Sporting Chance

You should have gone into football. 46 percent.

....

As an NBA head coach, what are the chances that I'll still be employed in this job at the beginning of next season?

69.1 percent.

....

What are the chances I'll make it to the major baseball leagues if I'm a first-round draft choice?

60 percent.

....

What are the chances a base runner will be caught trying to steal?

30 percent.

....

How likely is it that a field goal kick will succeed in professional football?

67 percent.

What are the chances the professional quarterback's passes will be completed?

55 percent.

....

What part of the professional football player's anatomy is at greatest risk of injury?

58 percent of all major injuries in professional football involve the knee.

....

Does playing offense or defense pose a greater risk of injury in professional football?

The risks are about equal. Special teams play, contrary to popular belief, is the safest.

....

Is it more dangerous playing football on artificial turf or the real stuff?

Just slightly more risky on the artificial stuff.

....

Am I at greater risk of spending money on lottery tickets if I make a lot of money or little money?

The more money you make the less likely you are to buy lottery tickets.

....

In which state lotteries do participants have the best/least chance of getting a return on their money?

Massachusetts is the most generous (59.5 percent return). Arizona is least generous with a 43.8 percent return.

....

Am I at greater risk of gambling if I'm a Catholic, a Christian fundamentalist, or an atheist?

Bingo—you got it: about 80 percent of all Catholics confess to gambling now and then, compared with only 33 percent of the fundamentalists, and 40 percent of the atheists.

....

Are favorites in horse races really good risks?

Compared with all the other horses, yes. They win approximately 36 percent of the time. The nags second favored come in first 22 percent of the time. Overall, bettors overbet the long shots (that is, they invest more money in long shots than is justified by the rate of success) and underbet the favorites—which is how horse racing stays in business.

WHAT ARE THE CHANCES?

As a regular racetrack bettor, will I actually make money in the long run?

From the horse's mouth: neigh. Fewer than 1 in 100 regulars actually make bucks at the track.

....

How much more likely am I to have the winning horse if my jockey is a pro rather than an apprentice?

Not at all more likely. Your chances, either way, are approximately equal.

....

What are the chances I'll actually make money, long-term, as a gambler?

Crappy. About 1 in 5,000 gamblers regularly turn a profit.

....

What is the chance that a professional poker player will resort to cheating?

Some "insiders" have estimated that 60 percent of Las Vegas pros and 40 percent of Gardenia, California, pros cheat at poker.

Sporting Chance

In poker, how much more likely is it that I will get a straight than a flush on the deal?

Your chances of being dealt a straight are about twice as good as your chances of getting a flush. You'll get a straight in 1 of every 255 hands dealt you, a flush in 1 of every 509 hands.

....

How often can I expect to be dealt a full house, four of a kind, a straight flush, or a royal flush in poker?

Don't stay up all night waiting. Your chances of getting the full house, on the deal, are 1 in 693, 1 in 4,164 for four of a kind, 1 in 72,192 for the straight flush, and 1 regal hand out of every 649,739 for the royal flush.

....

Okay, then, I'll settle for a pair, two pairs, or a triplet. What are my chances for those?

Get set for a pair, on the deal, every 2.4 hands, two pairs every 21 hands, three of a kind every 47 hands.

....

What are the chances I'll get a royal flush in two consecutive hands of poker?

Somewhat better than your chances of being killed in a plane crash.

....

In a full poker game, how likely is it that a pro will play up to and beyond the first bet?

Only about 25 percent. Pros spend most of their time *not* playing.

....

Overall, how much am I likely to win or lose, long-term, playing craps?

Overall you'll lose 16.7 percent of what you gamble. If you stick to playing the odds, however, you'll break even over the long haul (averaging all players).

....

How much of a risk is roulette compared with craps?

Overall, people lose more of what they gamble at craps than they do at roulette. Whereas they'll lose more than 16 percent of what they bet at craps, on average, they'll lose about 5 to 8 percent, again on average, of what they bet at the American roulette table.

Sporting Chance

If the dealer's up card, in blackjack, is an ace, what are the chances he/she will get blackjack?

Not bad. 31 percent.

....

How do the risks of blackjack compare with other games of chance?

Very well. In fact, even if you don't memorize cards but play with the "optimal strategy" you can easily learn from reading an authoritative book on the game, the odds are slightly in your favor: .5002 win versus .4998 lose. After a few years this heady profit margin should be enough to buy you a new deck of cards.